Sermons On The Second Readings

For Sundays In Advent, Christmas, And Epiphany

Gifts Of Thanksgiving

Richard Gribble, CSC

GIFTS OF THANKSGIVING
ADVENT/CHRISTMAS/EPIPHANY

Copyright © 2009 by
CSS Publishing Company, Inc.
Lima, Ohio

All rights reserved. No part of this publication may be reproduced in any manner whatsoever without the prior permission of the publisher, except in the case of brief quotations embodied in critical articles and reviews. Inquiries should be addressed to: Permissions, CSS Publishing Company, Inc., 517 South Main Street, Lima, Ohio 45804.

Some scripture quotations are from the New Revised Standard Version of the Bible, copyright 1989 by the Division of Christian Education of the National Council of the Churches of Christ in the USA. Used by permission.

Some scripture quotations are from the Holy Bible, New Living Translation, copyright © 1996. Used by permission of Tyndale House Publishers, Inc., Wheaton, Illinois 60189. All rights reserved.

Some scripture quotations are from the Revised Standard Version of the Bible, copyrighted 1946, 1952 ©, 1971, 1973, by the Division of Christian Education of the National Council of the Churches of Christ in the USA. Used by permission.

For more information about CSS Publishing Company resources, visit our website at www.csspub.com or email us at custserv@csspub.com or call (800) 241-4056.

Cover design by Barbara Spencer

ISSN: 1937-1454

ISBN-13: 978-0-7880-2652-2
ISBN-10: 0-7880-2652-6

PRINTED IN USA

Table Of Contents

**Sermons For Sundays
In Advent, Christmas, And Epiphany**
Gifts Of Thanksgiving
by Richard Gribble, CSC

Preface	7
Advent 1	11
Thanksgiving Means Giving	
1 Thessalonians 3:9-13	
Advent 2	17
Jesus — The Leader Of Our Team	
Philippians 1:3-11	
Advent 3	21
Rejoicing Brings Peace	
Philippians 4:4-7	
Advent 4	27
Obedience: Our Gift To Jesus	
Hebrews 10:5-10	
Christmas Eve/Christmas Day	33
Leading Others To Jesus	
Titus 2:11-14	
Christmas 1	39
Learning The Recipe For Love	
Colossians 3:12-17	

Christmas 2 45
    The Hidden Gifts Of Christ
    Ephesians 1:3-14

The Epiphany Of Our Lord 51
    Ambassadors Of The Lord
    Ephesians 3:1-12

The Baptism Of Our Lord 57
Epiphany 1
Ordinary Time 1
    Responsibility Comes With Privilege
    Acts 8:14-17

Epiphany 2 63
Ordinary Time 2
    Strength Through Diversity
    1 Corinthians 12:1-11

Epiphany 3 69
Ordinary Time 3
    Teammates In Building The Kingdom
    1 Corinthians 12:12-31a

Epiphany 4 75
Ordinary Time 4
    Love — The Basic Christian Call
    1 Corinthians 13:1-13

Epiphany 5 81
Ordinary Time 5
    The Great Sacrifice Of Love
    1 Corinthians 15:1-11

Epiphany 6   87
Ordinary Time 6
   Raised To New Life Today
   1 Corinthians 15:12-20

Epiphany 7   93
Ordinary Time 7
   Formula For Eternal Life
   1 Corinthians 15:35-38, 42-50

Epiphany 8   99
Ordinary Time 8
   Christ: The Victor Over Death
   1 Corinthians 15:51-58

Epiphany 9   105
Ordinary Time 9
   Don't Compromise Your Beliefs
   Galatians 1:1-12

The Transfiguration Of Our Lord   111
(Last Sunday After Epiphany)
   Transformed To Christ
   2 Corinthians 3:12—4:2

US/Canadian Lectionary Comparison   117

Preface

Giving and receiving gifts are activities in which we all participate. Gifts come in all shapes and sizes and are given for many reasons and on various occasions. Some gifts are very large, others are very small; yet their significance has nothing to do with their size. We give gifts to people on special occasions — birthdays, anniversaries, graduations, special achievements in life, and special holidays, such as Christmas. The reasons we give gifts vary, as well. Sometimes we want to celebrate milestones in our lives. Annually we celebrate with our friends on the day of their birth and their anniversary of commitment through marriage. We recognize major accomplishments in school, business, our work in the civic community, the military, or the church. We give gifts to demonstrate our love, care, and affection for special people in our lives. In such cases there is no need for a special occasion; the catalyst is the love that binds us to other individuals.

As we give gifts to each other, God has never ceased giving gifts to us. Each of us has received the gift of varied and multiple strengths. These manifest themselves through physical talents, the opportunities we enjoy in life, and the time necessary to properly utilize these great gifts in the promotion and building of God's kingdom in our world. All of us have been given certain material possessions. Some enjoy a great abundance of the fruits of the earth; some, unfortunately, have very little. Most of us, at least in the United States, find ourselves somewhere in the middle. God has given us a certain amount of power and prestige. We may hold it in our place of work, civic community where we live, the church we attend, or in the family of which we are members. Again, for some, power and prestige are significant, for others minimal, and for most, sufficient for their needs.

The Advent and Christmas seasons are a time for us to prepare and celebrate the Incarnation. God's greatest gift to the world, Jesus Christ, chose to come among us as a human being in order to set us free from all that binds us and keeps us prisoners. During this holy season we make many preparations to give gifts. In our society, however, we recall that it is our custom, when celebrating a birthday, to give gifts to the one whose anniversary or birth we remember. Therefore, as we prepare for and celebrate Christ's birth, we must ask ourselves, "What are we prepared to give to the newborn king of the Jews?" We all know that Christ wants and needs nothing of a material nature from us. There is nothing we could possibly conceive that God does not already possess. There is one thing, however, that the Lord desires and deserves from us. The best possible gift we can present to Christ is our fealty, commitment, and persistence in the Christian life. In other words, the greatest gift we can give to Christ is ourselves, seeking to be the best possible person we can. In short, Jesus wants our gift of thanksgiving. We are to give thanks to God for our lives and all that we have been given. We must live our lives in an attitude of thanksgiving to God.

The sermons in this volume speak of our thanksgiving to God. How is our thanksgiving to God manifest? Obviously, there is no one answer, but the second lesson scripture readings during these holy seasons provide us some insight. First, we learn that we must be giving people, to others and to God. Scripture teaches us that we must rejoice in God's presence and be obedient to God. Our call to be disciples and lead others to the Lord is an integral part of giving thanks to God. We also learn of our need to work with others in building the kingdom of God in our world. Overall, it is our thanksgiving to God through love, the element that binds all wonderful qualities together, that always must be evident in our lives.

The sermons in this book reflect my personal thanksgiving to God. How one expresses thanks is unique to the individual. My hope is that these reflections might resonate in some way, spark an idea or two in others, or serve as a catalyst to inspire the reader into asking, "What is my gift to the newborn king of the Jews?" God has and will continue to shower upon us varied and multiple gifts.

Now, especially during these holy seasons of Advent and Christmas, it is incumbent upon us to consider our response. Hopefully these reflections will assist the reader not only to ponder, but to respond in love to God, whose great love gave us the Incarnation, and to Jesus whose life, death, and resurrection brought us the possibility of eternal life.

— Richard Gribble, CSC

Advent 1
1 Thessalonians 3:9-13

Thanksgiving Means Giving

When Billy Walsh was a youngster, his family lived near Mrs. Smithson. A widow eighty years of age, Mrs. Smithson was in constant pain and crippled by rheumatoid arthritis that ravaged her body. Living alone she could only walk a few steps at a time with the help of her cane. Every week when Billy's mom went to the market, she took her son, who would always deliver groceries to the old widow. The family car would pull up into Mrs. Smithson's driveway and the command would be heard, "Billy, here are Mrs. Smithson's groceries." That was all the instruction that was needed. Billy instantly responded, delivering the groceries with a sense of delight. Without fail Mrs. Smithson always gave Billy a quarter for his efforts.

The boy enjoyed the older woman, especially listening to her stories. She told him about her life, a beautiful, old church in the woods, horse and buggy rides on Sunday afternoons, and much about her family's farm that had no modern conveniences such as electricity or running water. After a short time together the older woman would give Billy his quarter, which he would half-heartedly refuse, knowing that she would insist that he keep it. Usually he walked across the street to Johnson's candy store and bought himself a treat.

One day in mid-December Billy was delivering the woman's groceries as usual, but the season's first significant snow was falling and the boy very much wanted to go out and play. He decided, therefore, to make his delivery and refuse to accept Mrs. Smithson's weekly offering of 25 cents. The snow beckoned him to go outside.

Thus, Billy delivered the groceries much faster than normal. The older woman took the items out of the bag and told Billy where each went in the cabinets. Normally he enjoyed this, but the snow was calling. Then, somewhat suddenly Billy began to realize how lonely Mrs. Smithson must have been. She had been a widow for nearly twenty years and she had no children. Her only living relative, who never came to visit, lived far away in Boston. Nobody even called her at Christmas. When the holiday drew near, the house had no tree, no presents, and no stockings. For her, Christmas was just another day on the calendar. Billy began to think, *Maybe the snow could wait a bit; it wasn't that important.*

Billy and Mrs. Smithson sat and talked about many things but especially past Christmas celebrations. The journey of reflection and memories must have been somewhat healing for the older woman. Then she said, "Well, Billy, I bet you want to go out and play in the snow." She reached into her purse, fumbling to find the proper coin. "No, Mrs. Smithson," he said, "I cannot take your money this time. I am sure you have more important uses for it."

But she replied, "What more important thing could I do with it than give some to a friend at Christmas time?" She placed a silver dollar in Billy's hand. He tried to give it back, but she would have none of that.

Billy hurried out the door and ran to Johnson's candy store. He wondered what he would buy — a comic book, a chocolate soda, or ice cream. Then he spotted a Christmas card with an old country church on the cover. It was just like the church Mrs. Smithson had described from her youth. Billy purchased the card and borrowed a pen to sign his name. "Is this for your girlfriend?" Mr. Johnson asked. Billy started to say, "No," but responded, "Well, yeah, I guess it is."

He walked across the street and rang the widow's doorbell. He handed her the card, saying, "Merry Christmas, Mrs. Smithson. Thank you for your kindness."

The older woman's hand began to tremble as she opened the card and read its contents. She began to cry. "Thank you very much," and then in almost a whisper, "Merry Christmas to you."

Several weeks later, one cold and blustery day, an ambulance arrived at Mrs. Smithson's home. Mrs. Walsh, Billy's mother, told her son that she had found Mrs. Smithson in bed; she had died peacefully in her sleep. On her nightstand was found, still illuminated by a light, a solitary Christmas card with an old country church on the cover.

This story, set during the Christmas season, provides a perfect entrée to the Advent period, which the church begins today. In essence the story is one of thanksgiving, the young boy's thanksgiving to the woman and her thanksgiving to him. Our second lesson, drawn from 1 Thessalonians, presents us with a message of thanksgiving, but one that is specific in giving thanks through giving.

Saint Paul wrote 1 Thessalonians, most probably the first letter of his corpus, approximately in the year 50 AD. He had founded the Christian community at Thessalonica during his second missionary journey (Acts 17:1-9). In the short passage we heard proclaimed, the apostle offers thanks to the Thessalonians. He is grateful for them and the faith they have demonstrated, but he wants to suggest certain ways that thanksgiving must be manifest.

First, Paul suggests that thanksgiving must be an act of presence; he believes we demonstrate thanks to each other by being physically present with one another. As a nation, we in the United States have just completed the celebration of our national day of Thanksgiving. Most people gathered with families and friends; we were present to each other. We intentionally sought to be with these people at this special time. Many people traveled great distances; one might say we went out of our way to be present to special people in our lives. We made these journeys joyfully because these are people we know and love; there was no great strain to be physically present with these people. We welcomed the opportunity.

However, Paul's concept of presence as an action of thanksgiving requires more of us. Being an excellent judge of human character, Paul realized that to be present to people we know, like, or perceive can be of advantage to us is not difficult at all. He realized the need, and so must we, to move beyond being present simply to those we like, but in an act of thanksgiving, to be present to those we know and possibly do not like. I suspect at the outset Billy was not too pleased to be present to Mrs. Smithson, as it would take him away from his friends. But he learned about the importance of being present, especially to those who needed him most. Equally importantly he discovered the peace and beauty that came to him through his act of thanksgiving. He found that he was serving not only the individual, but God who gives us the opportunity to be present and serve.

Being present can manifest itself in many different ways. We need to take up the challenge and be thankful by visiting a neighbor, a colleague at work, or a member of our church community who is sick, whether in the hospital or at home. Taking the time that we seemingly do not possess to be present with another and simply sit and listen is a great gift, almost a lost art in today's world. Many times all people need is simply a compassionate ear. We need to be present with the elderly, family members most assuredly, but also those we know in various ways. We need to be present for special events — birthdays, anniversaries, and weddings. But the everyday events, being present for meals, sporting events of children, and family time together is essential. Paul is asking the Thessalonians to be present to each other and thereby demonstrate thanksgiving. The same is true for us.

A second aspect of Saint Paul's concept of thanksgiving is mutual love. He writes, "May the Lord make you increase and abound in love for one another and for all, just as we abound in love for you" (1 Thessalonians 3:12). As the first season of the new liturgical year, Advent presents us the opportunity for new beginnings, to start afresh in demonstrating mutual love. If we are at odds with someone it is the perfect time to once again demonstrate the love to which all Christians are called. Jesus never held a grudge. In fact, we recall his words on the cross, "Father, forgive them for they do not know what they are doing" (Luke 23:34). Disagreements arise within families, coworkers, neighbors, and even within our church communions. Paul's words encourage us to "drop the hatchet" and move toward reconciliation and love. Still we must go further. We must reach across borders and boundaries that separate and drive people apart. Racial and ethnic divisions, national boundaries, and even religious denominations and teachings keep us from being the mutually loving people that is part of Paul's thanksgiving message to the Thessalonians.

Instead of division and strife we should offer love as the concept of belonging, unity, and harmony. A thanksgiving of mutual love requires us to be inclusive in all we do and say. Jesus continually crossed borders, both literally and figuratively, to demonstrate an inclusive ethic with all people. He visited lands and cities outside Israel, such as Tyre, Sidon, and the Gerasene Territory. He never shied away from lepers, cripples, the blind, or others with physical handicaps. On the contrary, he embraced these people, demonstrating an ethic of being inclusive.

Rather than being inclusive, too often people in contemporary life are exclusive. We choose our friends, opportunities, and associations with great care. Only certain people or possibilities that pass our personal litmus test show up on our radar screens. People are chosen based on their attributes, skills, and the possibilities they bring in our lives. Opportunities similarly are chosen if they will advance our personal or professional lives or serve us in an advantageous way. The thanksgiving effort of mutual love that Paul preaches to the Thessalonians is completely antithetical to such an exclusive way of thinking or acting.

Paul's third aspect of thanksgiving is proper conduct. He writes, "May he so strengthen your hearts in holiness that you may be blameless before our God and Father at the coming of our Lord Jesus Christ with all his saints" (1 Thessalonians 3:13). The new start that Advent brings challenges us to transform our lives of faith and make them more conformable to that of Christ. We should use this time to root out vices that ill-affect our health — smoking, overheating, excessive drinking, or laziness. It is a time to cast out hatred, jealousy, pride, and arrogance, those things that create violence in our lives, and replace them with justice, goodness, humility, kindness, and those things that generate peace. In short, we must root out actions that are inconsistent with our common Christian vocation to holiness. As a Christian hymn goes, "Let there be peace on earth and let it begin with me." We must find peace in our hearts by doing what is right. Right conduct leads directly to peace within our hearts.

There is a short little story that aptly illustrates this point. One day a young man answered a want ad for a farm hand. He told the owner about his previous experience, which was abundant, and his references were impeccable. He ended the interview in a rather odd way, however, by telling the owner that he could count on him, because he could sleep during the wind. The owner was confused but he could not argue with the man's credentials so he was given the job.

Late one night a fierce Midwest storm arose. It was two in the morning but the farmer arose, got dressed, and went outside to see what needed to be secured. First, he checked the barn, but the doors were closed, shutters were locked tight, and the animals were tethered and safe. He next checked the springhouse, the pump room, and storage shed, and all the trucks. Everything was secured. He ran from place to place thinking most assuredly that something must be out of order. Finally, the owner stuck his head in the bunkhouse and saw the farmhand fast asleep. He remembered the curious statement of the farmhand when he was interviewed, "I can sleep during the wind." The farmer smiled and thought to himself, "Yes, he is at peace and has done all things well. He can sleep during the wind."

As we begin a new liturgical year by lighting the first candle on the Advent wreath, Saint Paul encourages us to manifest an attitude of thanksgiving. While saying "thank you" in a physical sense is a start, we must go further. Paul tells the Thessalonians that he is grateful to them, but now they must demonstrate an ethic of thanksgiving of presence, mutual love, and right conduct to others. Similarly, we need to manifest thanksgiving in our lives. People need us to be present to them; they have the right to our love and respect. Society and God challenge us to reform our lives more along that of Jesus Christ. Let our Advent journey begin by being thankful. Our attitude can be so simply and succinctly stated, as articulated by Saint Ignatius of Loyola, "May all we do and say give greater glory and honor to God." Amen.

Advent 2
Philippians 1:3-11

Jesus – The Leader Of Our Team

One day a young girl came home from school in tears because she had only been given a small part in the school play, while her classmate and best friend had received the lead role. After drying the girl's eyes, her mother took off her watch, put it in her hand, and said, "What do you see?" The girl replied, "A gold band, the watch face, and two hands." Then the mother flipped the watch over, opened the back, and again asked her daughter, "Now, what do you see?" The little girl looked closely at all the internal watch mechanisms and saw many little wheels, springs, and other small pieces. The mother explained, "This watch would be useless without every part — even the tiny ones you can hardly see." The young girl always remembered her mother's lesson to realize that all must work together to make any operation function well.

The lesson the young girl learned from her mother is an important lesson for all of us who seek to follow Jesus, our leader in the faith. As the various components of the watch — some large, others small, some seemingly important, and others of lesser importance — must all work together for the watch to function, so too, must the Christian community work together as one, under the leadership of Christ, to further his message and to bring his peace to an oftentimes troubled world.

As with the second lesson last week from 1 Thessalonians, today's lesson is taken from the "thanksgiving" section of Paul's letter to the Philippians. Saint Paul speaks of the need to work as a team, headed by Christ, to bring Jesus' message to people of the region. He speaks generally of the mutuality of love and care that must reign in the community; he urges the people to remain pure and blameless in God's eyes. Yet, he goes much further, raising another highly significant concept, the idea of sharing through Jesus, the central figure of our faith. Paul is thankful because the Philippians hold him in their hearts as he does them. He longs for the community and wants to be an integral part of their life of faith. Yet, while this is important, he says it is secondary to sharing in God's grace. Paul wants the Philippians to be a community but only with Jesus as the hub, the central figure.

Clearly Paul, from his own conversion, understood the necessity of the centrality of Jesus in his life. When he heard Jesus' voice on the road, he knew the rest of his life would be centered on him. He had no idea at the time what this would mean and how much he would have to sacrifice, but he fully knew there was no way he could conduct his life without Jesus as his central guiding figure. Thus, for Paul, finding our way to life eternal is not only the goal, but Jesus is the way to achieve that lofty pinnacle.

The gospels, both the synoptic writers and John, affirm what Paul was telling the Philippians, namely the need to center our lives on Christ, his message, and his way of life. In the Sermon on the Mount, Jesus challenges his followers to follow the narrow, rougher, and less-traveled path, but the only one that leads to life,

> *Enter through the narrow gate; for the gate is wide and the road is easy that leads to destruction, and there are many who take it. For the gate is narrow and the road is hard that leads to life, and there are few who find it.*
> — Matthew 7:13-14

Saint John is unique among the gospel evangelists in the many titles he gives to Jesus. He describes Jesus as, "the way, the truth and the life," "the Bread of Life," the "door," and "gate." The powerful image of the vine and branches well illustrates the centrality of Jesus: "I am the vine, you are the branches. Those who abide in me and I in them bear much fruit, because apart from me you can do nothing" (John 15:5). Scripture clearly shows how Jesus is the central figure for our personal lives and our community of faith.

Too often, however, Jesus is forced to take a backseat to people and ideas that compete for our attention. The need for a central figure in our lives of faith is made quite obvious when we see the absolute need for a unifying part, person, or ideal that serves to hold together things without unity. Take, for example, the hub at the center of a bicycle wheel. Each of the spokes of a wheel has importance, giving structure and strength, yet it is the hub that holds the spokes and thus the wheel together. Similarly, sports teams have many players but there is always a central figure or goal to hold a team together. Teams have managers and head coaches; they have goals such as the World Series in baseball, the Super Bowl in football, and the Stanley Cup in hockey. In families, while there are many members, it is the parents who stand at the hub and hold the family together, whether that is a nuclear or extended one.

As with other institutions of society, our churches also must seek unity and centrality. We have our pastors, bishops, and other central figures. These people are very important but only to the degree that they help lead us to the ultimate central figure who is Jesus Christ. The Bible is very clear about what Jesus asks of us and how he must be the central figure of our lives; yet we somehow believe we know more or better and seek another figure. When this happens we soon become lost.

The consequences that come to communities that refuse to have a centralizing ideal or person are quite obvious; they are manifest in varied ways in our world. If the spokes of a wheel do not have the hub there would be no central strength and the wheel would not function. In sports and even in families, when one desires to move out on one's own, breaking unity, disaster is not far off. In families this can be manifest through lack of discipline. It may be children who "do their own thing," parents who are unfaithful, or individuals who seek solace in things that lead nowhere — drugs, alcohol, and gambling. The list goes on and on.

In our churches we live in a fragile belief system or at least so it seems! Our churches have certain rules and regulations; there are certain ways of operating. Yet, individualism seems to have such a strong pull on our loyalties that we feel free to believe what we want and basically to do what we wish. Self-autonomy trumps the community. Such attitudes are present on all fronts. We can see it in individual parishes, local dioceses, and even our international communions. We have moved away from the centrality of Jesus, the door, the gate, the rough and narrow path, and have chosen to take alternate routes. But, as certain as the wheel does not function without the centrality of the hub, or the watch without all the parts working together, so too, our faith communities and our churches will not function well without our common focus on the centrality of Christ. The created world seeks unity; the parts of the watch must work together. Similarly God's greatest creation, the human race, must not only seek but find unity. We must work together to produce the desired result we seek.

A simple yet humorous story well illustrates our need for each other. A world-renowned organist was giving a performance at a local church using a huge, antique organ for his concert. It used a bellows for its pipes. The bellows was hand-pumped by a boy who was behind the screen, unseen by the audience. The first half of the concert, which featured the music of Johann Sebastian Bach, was well received by the audience. All in attendance were thrilled by the organist's ability at the keyboard of this beautiful instrument. After taking his bows and accepting the ovation of the audience, the famous musician walked triumphantly offstage by a side passageway. As he passed by, the boy who was pumping the bellows said, "We played well, didn't we, sir?" The famous musician rather haughtily replied, "And what do you mean by we? I was the one playing the music. I was the one whose ability was recognized by the audience."

After intermission, the organist returned to his seat at the impressive five-keyboard console and began to play. But nothing happened; not a sound was heard. Then the organist heard a youthful voice whisper from behind the screen, "Hey, mister, do you know what *we* means now?"

Let us, therefore, as individuals and a community of faith take Saint Paul's advice and follow the road to unity and find our life in Jesus our leader. Such obedience will place us on the train that leads to God and life eternal. Amen.

Advent 3
Philippians 4:4-7

Rejoicing Brings Peace

Mora Naba, a Mossi emperor in Burkina Faso, had conquered a powerful ethnic group in the south called the Kaesena. He extracted tribute from them once each year. One year, at tribute collecting time, the emperor made the mistake of sending his son, Nabiiga, a prince and his heir apparent. When the Kaesena saw Nabiiga with only a very small entourage of guardians, they overpowered the group and took the prince hostage.

His kingly robes were stripped from him, and he was forced to walk around in only a loincloth. The prisoner received only one meal per day and was forced out into the fields each morning to work. Normally, manual labor would be beneath the dignity of royalty, so the Kaesena made great sport of him. The women would pass by and belittle him. While he was working in the fields, the children would throw pebbles and stones at him.

But, to the great surprise of all those watching from day to day, the Mossi prince would work and sing. He sang cheerfully with a loud voice as he worked from sun up to sun down. At first his soft hands blistered and then bled as he was unaccustomed to using farm equipment. He lost significant weight, but he continued to be cheerful and to sing.

The elders of the Kaesena were much troubled by his singing and buoyant attitude. "How can he possibly sing," they would continually ask, "since we make him sleep on the ground and make sport of him each day? We give him very little food, and he is forced to labor from sun up to sun down. Our women and our children mock him, but he continues to sing!"

After a month of watching, they finally called him before a council. He stood in his loincloth straight and proud in their midst. The elder spokesperson for the Kaesena people asked the Mossi prince about his behavior: "Why do you sing?" Nabiiga answered, "It is true. You've taken away my fine clothes. You have made me work, you give me very little food to eat, and you make me sleep on the ground in a common hut. You have tried to take away all my pride and all my earthly possessions. You have brought great shame upon me. Now you ask me why, in spite of all this, I can sing. I can sing because you cannot take away my title and who I am. I am Moro Naba's first son. I am proud of that and will never react to your shameful behavior!"

The Kaesena people learned that they could not bring shame upon the Mossi prince because he was at peace and, therefore, could continue to sing. The peace that the prince felt inside was an active virtue manifest in his behavior; peace was not simply the absence of violence and war in his life. To become peacemakers, as the story suggests, we must proactively act and speak. As we light the third candle on the Advent wreath and know by the calendar, as well as Saint Paul's words, that Jesus is near, we must consider our response to the challenge to rejoice and, thereby, bring peace.

The Advent journey we have been traveling the last three weeks, a time of expectation and waiting, has concentrated on the second coming of Jesus and the ministry of John the Baptist. Today, however, we start to concentrate on the arrival of Jesus in time — the Incarnation. The Jews had waited many centuries since the prophecy of Isaiah, Jeremiah, Micah, and their predictions of a messiah. The Jews fully expected a great king who would restore the greatness of Israel as during the time of David. The Roman occupation of the land would end; the greatness of Israel would once again shine to all nations.

While we realize that the messiahship and kingdom that Jesus brought were far different from what the Jews expected, it is still a time of great rejoicing that the Lord is near. What Jesus brought is far more important than expectations of power and greatness, which dominated the thinking and hopes of the Jews. We must rejoice because we know, based on many factors, of the close proximity of

Jesus. First, the calendar tells us that December 25 is not far off. We cannot go very far in any mode of transportation without encountering some physical manifestation of Christmas — decorations, traffic at the malls, and billboards that announce sales. We hear Christmas carols on the radio, our mailboxes are filled with cards and other greetings from friends and family, and we are bombarded by commercials on television for all the latest things that various stories and retailers want us to buy for our friends and loved ones.

Scripture, too, informs us of the Lord's proximate arrival. Yes, we have the words of John the Baptist who speaks of the need to prepare for this great event. In today's second lesson Paul, writing to the Christian community at Philippi, suggests our preparation must include great rejoicing, because the Lord is near.

We all know how to rejoice with great fervor when things go right, and we are in control and on top of the situation. This is a rather natural reaction when our success is personal, that of one we know and love, or even that of an organization to which we have loyalty. We rejoice in our personal and family successes, the triumph of a friend over obstacles or disease. We rejoice when our favorite college or professional sports team wins the big game or even a championship.

Saint Paul tells us today that there is another element of rejoicing. He suggests we need to eliminate our propensity to worry and replace our anxiety with prayer and supplications to God. As a society we like to worry. In fact, we have a whole industry associated with it. When we worry we seek resolution through medications and various professionals. Certainly what medical science collectively has done for us with respect to our penchant to worry is laudable and generally helpful, but we worry far too much. Naturally we worry about our family: our children, our finances, our health, and our future. But, as we know, there are some people who prefer to worry; they do not seem content under any other mode of operation.

Paul suggests we must cast our cares on the Lord by substituting prayer and supplication to God instead of manifesting our worries and concerns. This sounds good, but we know it is not easy to accomplish. We want, like the Kaesena people, to find some answer to our concerns, to our lack of peace, but Paul suggests that if we trust God and let our prayer take the place of our worry, the elusive peace we ultimately seek will be ours. The author of the book of Proverbs was correct when he wrote: "Trust in the Lord with all your heart, and do not rely on your own insight" (Proverbs 3:5). Paul says that the peace of God, which surpasses all our understanding, will guard our hearts and minds. This peace is certainly a reality we all seek — to feel at peace and know that God will guard our hearts and minds to the attainment of this goal.

Scripture and tradition have provided Jesus with numerous titles, each of which resonates with certain people at different times. The image of Jesus as the good shepherd presents the Lord as the compassionate one who seeks out the lost, even going so far as to leave 99 perfectly good sheep to fend for themselves while he searches for us, the one who is lost. When Jesus describes himself as "the way, the truth, and the life," he helps us understand that he is the guide to all that we need, all that will sustain us. Jesus' description of himself as the vine and we as the branches, expressing our need to always remain connected to him, brings us both consolation and challenge. It is a challenge for we must follow and stay connected, but if we do, we have the promise that where Jesus resides we will one day be. The image of Jesus as the "Bread of Life" (John 6) helps us to know that he is our spiritual sustenance. We can always go to him with any and all needs.

Isaiah's image of the Messiah as the "Prince of Peace" (Isaiah 9:5), is especially relevant as we draw closer to Christmas. Our troubled world, with so much hatred, violence, and armed conflict, badly needs the peace that only Christ can bring. This peace must be active, however; it is never passive. Pope Paul VI put it so succinctly, "If you want peace, work for justice." Peace will only come when we actively seek it. Thus, we must cooperate with Jesus, the Prince of Peace, to assure that Christ's peace will be manifest in the world. The apostle suggests that the way we can bring peace is by being joyful people. Rejoicing truly can bring peace.

Rejoicing must become a way of life, not simply a momentary respite from our general worrisome and dour countenance. We cannot win every game; we don't always hit home runs. But, if we continue to play the game, if we never give up, we can rejoice that God is with us. As we draw closer to our Advent goal, as the signs, smells, and sounds of Christmas draw near, let us as Paul suggests, "Rejoice in the Lord always; again I will say, Rejoice" (v. 4a). Our spirit will bring us peace, and peace will bring us and our world one step closer to God and life eternal. Amen.

Advent 4
Hebrews 10:5-10

Obedience: Our Gift To Jesus

One day a man went to his son's bedroom and found him sitting on his bed with a whole stack of comic books around him. The father said to his son, "Matthew, where did you get the comic books?"

Matthew responded, "I took them out of the library."

"You took them out of the library? You mean you stole them from the library?"

The boy responded, "Yes."

The father called the library and said he was going to march his son immediately down with the comic books to apologize and to restore all he had stolen. After returning from the library he gave Matthew a stern lecture about stealing.

The following summer, the family took its vacation in a small community in Vermont where there was a general store. When they returned home after the summer, the father went into Matthew's room and again found a pile of comic books in his dresser drawer. Matthew this time admitted, "I stole them from the store in the summer."

This time the father took the comic books and started a fire in the fireplace. He threw the comic books into the flames and with each comic book they threw in, he reminded his son of the seventh commandment, "Thou shall not steal."

One year later, Matthew again stole some comic books and this time his father told Matthew he was going to have to spank him. He brought him into the study, put him over his knee, and spanked him quite soundly. While he did not want to hurt his son, he did want to teach him a significant lesson. After this session he sat down and wanted to talk with his son. It was obvious that Matthew did not want to shed a tear in front of his father. The father understood that and, so as not to ruin the boy's pride, said, "Matthew, I am going to leave you alone for a while, but I will be back in a few minutes."

The father then stepped out of the room and closed the door behind him. He himself began to cry and to do so in a manner that was quite obvious to his son behind the door. After a few minutes he regained his composure, went to the bathroom, washed his face, and then returned to his son's room to speak with him.

Years later, when Matthew was a teenager and he was with his mother driving back from a shopping trip, the two were reminiscing as parents and children often do. Matthew began to retell the story of when he was a youngster and often stole comic books. He said to his mother, "You know, after that incident with Dad, I never stole another thing."

His mother commented, "I suppose the reason was because your father spanked you."

"Oh, no," replied Matthew, "it was because when he stepped out of the room I could hear him crying."

Matthew's mother thought her son had learned a lesson in obedience from the punishment he received at the hands of his father, but she learned to her surprise that he learned this hard lesson in life through the pain he inflicted on his father. All the things Matthew could have done to bring his father joy — achievements such as straight A's in school, getting the winning basket or hit to bring a sports team a victory, or winning the local town's citizenship award — could not be measured against simply being obedient.

Obedience seems like such an easy task, yet in our contemporary world, which concentrates on self-promotion, being obedient is difficult. We learn the same lesson on this fourth Sunday of Advent. What Christ desires for a present on Christmas Day is not gold, frankincense, and myrrh, or any other material thing. What Jesus wants and can expect from us is our obedience — to be the best person we can possibly be.

The letter to the Hebrews, from which today's second lesson is drawn, has an interesting place in the New Testament corpus. Initially this letter was thought to be part of Saint Paul's writings, but scholars today almost universally agree that the apostle to the Gentiles did not pen this document. More likely a Jewish Christian with a Hellenistic background wrote the letter as a mini theological treatise for a broad audience of people. The language, form, and theology of the letter all testify to a non-Pauline authorship. The importance of the letter is, however, equally uncontested, especially its references to Christ's new covenant. Jesus, according to the letter to the Hebrews, is the capstone, the fulfillment of the Hebrew scripture, who came to complete the law and lead the Christian community in a new direction.

As we have heard proclaimed, the letter places strong emphasis on the rejection of sacrifices and offerings and the need to substitute in their place obedience to God's will. We learn an important lesson, similar to that which Matthew's father, somewhat accidentally, taught his son. The father thought Matthew would learn obedience as a result of the punishment he received for his failures to follow the older man's exhortation to refrain from stealing. But the boy learned the lesson more profoundly by how his action hurt his father.

Similarly, the author of Hebrews tells us that outward actions of sacrifice and cereal offerings, which were so common to the Israelites in the desert and offerings of priests in the temple, are not what God seeks. Surely to perform such acts in a prayerful spirit was good and well-intentioned, and they were not to be condemned or rejected. However, Jesus, the new Adam, desires a new sign of love, the obedience of his people.

> *Sacrifices and offerings you have not desired, but a body you have prepared for me; in burnt offerings and sin offerings you have taken no pleasure.... I have come to do your will, O God.* — Hebrews 10:5b-7a

We learn that Jesus' arrival, the great event we await, abolishes the first idea, namely that of sacrifice and offerings, and establishes a second, the idea of obedience. The perfect example is the obedience of Christ himself to the will of his Father by offering his own body. Jesus' sacrifice, in obedience to his Father's will, transformed the world, bringing us the possibility of salvation.

The Christmas season, upon whose doorstep we now rest, celebrates the Incarnation, God becoming human in Jesus Christ, our Lord and redeemer. In our society when we celebrate a birthday, it is customary to give a gift to the person so honored. We need to reflect and consider, therefore, what our gift will be to the newborn king of the Jews. In short, as stated earlier, Jesus is not interested in anything we can buy or make, but he is very interested in seeing us attain the fullness of our Christian call, to be the person God wants us to be. Today, the author of the letter to the Hebrews suggests the best possible gift we can give to Jesus is our obedience.

Society today creates many difficulties, roadblocks, and barriers that hinder us from being obedient people. As a society we stress the individual, self-accomplishment, individual awards, and honors. Competition is endemic to every facet of our society. At times we are all quite bullheaded; we want our way and no other. We believe that everybody else must change to accommodate our needs. We are not willing to move or change course.

A little story appropriately illustrates how we often behave and how such actions could be disastrous. A battleship had been at sea on maneuvers in heavy weather for several days. The visibility was poor with patchy fog, so the captain remained on the bridge keeping an eye on all activities. Shortly after dark, the lookout on the wing of the bridge reported, "Light, bearing on the starboard bow."

The captain called out, "Is it steady or moving astern?"

The lookout replied, "The light is steady, captain."

Realizing that the situation was a collision course, the captain shouted to the radio man, "Send a message, we are on a collision course. Advise you change course 20° to port."

Almost immediately a reply was received, "Advise that you change course 20° to port."

Angrily the captain ordered a second message: "I am the ship's captain. Change course 20° to port now!"

Again, a reply came, "I am seaman second class, but you better change course immediately."

By this time the captain was furious. He ordered, "Send this message: This is a battleship; change your course immediately."

Back in a flash came the reply: "This is a lighthouse!" The battleship changed course. If we are unwilling to change course in our lives we may find ourselves in extremis or experience a collision with dire ramifications.

Many people today see obedience as restrictive and problematic. We feel we sacrifice too much to be obedient. Yet, obedience is what gives us freedom. Can any of us imagine our society without the obedience of law? While the law seems to restrict our freedom, it actually provides a structure for our society. If we obey the law then we find freedom. Similarly following the rules or keeping the regimen of the team brings discipline, esprit de corps, and triumph in sports. While there are individual stars on the various school and professional sports teams, it is the team that wins or loses. Those who act and play like a team in obedience, generally find themselves on the victorious side of any contest.

Similarly obedience to God and meeting our responsibilities and duties brings the peace that only God can bring. The story of a holy monk and a decision he was forced to make illustrates my point. There was an old and holy monk who prayed many years for a vision from God to strengthen his faith, but it never came. He had almost given up hope when, one day, a vision appeared. The monk was overjoyed. Then, right in the middle of the vision, the monastery bell rang that meant that it was time to feed the poor who gathered daily at the monastery gate.

Coincidentally it was the old monk's turn to feed them. He realized that if he failed to show up with food, the poor would leave quietly, thinking the monastery had nothing to give them that day. The monk was torn between earthly duty and the heavenly vision. However, before the bell stopped tolling the monk had made his decision. With a heavy heart, he turned his back on the vision and went off to feed the poor.

Nearly an hour later, the old monk returned to his room. To his great surprise and joy when he opened the door he saw the vision of God was still there waiting for him. The monk dropped to his knees in thanksgiving. God said to him, "My son, had you not gone off to feed the poor, I would not have stayed."

As we light the fourth candle on the Advent wreath and make our final preparations for the celebration of Christmas, let us consider what we need to do to be more obedient — to the people and the ideas of our society, but most especially to Christ. Let us realize that what Jesus desires and deserves from us this Christmas is an attitude of obedience to his will. We can present him with no more significant gift. Let us not disappoint him. Amen.

**Christmas Eve/Christmas Day
Titus 2:11-14**

Leading Others To Jesus

It was the Christmas season and thus the time for the local elementary school to present its annual Christmas play. One little girl named Caitlin invited her parents to come to the performance. She told them, "Mom and Dad, please come to the play for I have the most important role in the entire production." Of course, Caitlin's parents were more than happy to accept their daughter's invitation to attend the event.

On the night of the performance the school auditorium was filled with family, friends, and other well-wishers who looked forward to the annual Christmas play. As the curtain was drawn back from the stage the audience initially beheld Joseph leading a donkey across the stage, with Mary astride. The narrator told the story of how Caesar Augustus had ordered a census of the whole world, and it was necessary for Joseph to travel with Mary, his pregnant wife, to Bethlehem to register. Upon their arrival the couple looked for a place to stay but could find no room in the local inn.

As the play continued, Caitlin's parents wondered where their daughter was. Based on what she had said, they were sure that she would have the role of Mary or one of the shepherds, but so far she had not been present on stage. Then the narrator spoke of the birth of Jesus and with this a brilliant star arose over the stable to mark the spot of Jesus' birth. Caitlin was carrying the star above her head. Wherever Mary went with Jesus in her arms, Caitlin followed behind; the star never left Jesus.

When the play concluded all in attendance and the participants gathered in the cafeteria for a celebration of cookies, cake, and beverages. Caitlin asked her parents, "Did you enjoy the play?"

Her parents responded, "We loved it; it was great!"

Her father continued, "Caitlin you told us that you had one of the leading roles but we noticed that you carried the star. We thought you might be Mary or possibly one of the shepherds or magi."

Caitlin responded, "I had the most important role. It was my task as the star to lead others to Jesus. There could not be any more important task and privilege in the entire world."

In many ways the average person might see Caitlin's role in the play as secondary, even of little importance. Yet, she insisted her role was not only essential, but the most significant, because she had responsibility of leading others to the Lord. As the world today welcomes the newborn king of the Jews, we must realize that while we bask in the glory of God made man, God chose to become human like us in all things but sin. We, as Christians, bear a significant responsibility. The Pauline author of the letter to Titus tells us that we must do our part by leading upstanding lives, to be an example, and thereby lead others to Christ. It is a responsibility we must not fail to engage, to be the best person our abilities will allow us to be.

The letter to Titus, along with 1 and 2 Timothy comprising the so-called Pastoral Epistles, form a unique part of the New Testament. Biblical experts are uncertain as to the authorship of these letters, but, as with the letter to the Hebrews, differences in language and theology lead many exegetes to doubt authentic Pauline authorship. However, the message of the letter to Titus, as we just heard proclaimed, is highly significant.

The central missive of the passage tells us that the grace of God has appeared bringing salvation to all people. We know that the Christmas story is central to God's plan of salvation history. From the time God called Abraham, through the formation of the Israelite people, the great exodus, the periods of the two kingdoms of Israel and Judah and the prophets, and even the infamous Babylonian exile, God continued to provide evidence to the fact that a plan was in progress to bring God's people the gift of eternal life. Jesus' arrival in history begins the process that leads to his salvific death and resurrection.

The Pauline author of Titus says that while we await the manifestation of God's glory, to be made present upon Jesus' return, we have several significant responsibilities. We are initially called to renewal and to cast out worldly passions. The message of Christ must have a significant bearing on our lives. We must demonstrate in our lives of faith that the message of Christ has made a difference. Worldly passions are an everyday enticement. The allure of the created world is strong. Since the attraction of the world is so strong and pervasive, we must overtly choose to take another route.

This new path requires us to be countercultural, to place value on things of God and faith over the materialism of the world. People will think us odd, even foolish in our rejection of what the majority of our first-world society considers indispensable, yet this is precisely what being countercultural means. We must be a sign in an alienated world of a value system that is contrary to that of the world. Such a stance will require courage because the rewards that are so readily apparent and tangible for those who choose the world are hidden and latent for the Christian who chooses to shun worldly ties. Yet, our faith teaches us of the necessity of holding fast. Saint Paul puts it powerfully and beautifully in 1 Corinthians 2:9: "No eye has seen, nor ear heard, nor the human heart conceived, what God has prepared for those who love him."

As Caitlin brought others to Christ through her role as the "star" in the play, so we must lead others by the example we set. Paul tells us in the present age, and thus for all ages, we are to live self-controlled, upright, and godly lives. In other words we must live lives consistent with our Christian vocation. We are to set an example that others would want to follow. If that life is consistent with Christ's message then we become a beacon of light, like the star, which draws others to Christ. We, like those who felt Caitlin's role was minimal, might think that setting an example is a rather passive and small role in God's plan, but nothing could be farther from the truth.

Jesus came into our world, as we celebrate today, to bring light, hope, and to show us how to lead our lives in a way that is pleasing to God. He came to fulfill and complete the law, initiated on Mount Sinai with Moses. Christ did his share, but the work was only initiated during his life. We, his followers, have the privilege and responsibility to continue his work in our world.

Jesus is the light who comes to dispel the darkness. We must carry the light in a proactive way. We must be willing to take some risks in providing the light to others. We cannot abdicate this serious responsibility nor think we are not qualified to be Christ's representatives in our world. We must avoid the hesitation and reticence that, if we are not careful, can creep into our lives.

A little story illustrates this challenge. Three wise men were encouraged to find and explore what many called the cave of wisdom and life. They made careful preparations for what would be a challenging and arduous journey. When they reached the cave, they noted a guard stood at the entrance. They were not permitted to enter the cave until they had spoken with the guard. He had only one question for them, and he demanded that they answer only after talking it over amongst themselves. He assured them they would have a good guide to lead them through the regions of the cave. His question was a simple one, "How far into the cave of wisdom and life do you wish to go?"

The three travelers discussed the matter and then returned to the guard saying that they only wanted to go a very short distance, only so far as to say that they had been there. The response of the guard manifested great disappointment as he summoned someone to lead the three seekers a short distance into the cave and then watched them set out again after a very short time.

The three travelers were hesitant and were not willing to risk in order to find wisdom and knowledge. I am sure that Jesus will be equally disappointed in us, as was the guard of the cave, if we refuse to move forward and to use the talent, time, energy, and opportunities we have been given to bring the Lord's message to the world.

The Advent season, a period of patient expectation, has ended and today we welcome Jesus, the light, the Prince of Peace, and our source of salvation. As we rejoice in the Incarnation and the great privileges initiated for us who bear the name of Christian, we must always be mindful that responsibility is an essential element of the Christian life. The letter to Titus today suggests our need to be countercultural, to move away from the teachings of the world's passions, materialism, and self-autonomy, which twenty-first-century America tells us is normative, and seek instead an attitude of community and greater simplicity of life.

Additionally, we are challenged to exercise self-control and to live upright lives according to the message that Jesus proclaimed. In other words, we are called to be good examples, to be the light of Christ to others. Our words, actions, and attitudes should bring people closer to Christ. It is an awesome and extremely important responsibility. As we celebrate the arrival of the light that no darkness can overcome, let us be the light to others. May the miracle of the Incarnation, God made man, transform our lives forever! Amen.

Christmas 1
Colossians 3:12-17

Learning The Recipe For Life

In ancient times, a king decided to find and honor the greatest person among his subjects. A man of wealth and property was singled out. Another was praised for his healing powers and a third for his wisdom and knowledge of the law. Still another was lauded for his business acumen. Many other successful people were brought to the palace, and it became evident that the task of choosing the greatest would be difficult.

Finally the last candidate stood before the king. This woman had white hair and her eyes shone with the light of knowledge, understanding, and love.

"Who is this?" asked the king. "What has she done?"

"You have seen and heard all the others," said the king's aide. "This one is their teacher!"

With this the people all applauded and the king came down from his throne to honor her as the greatest of his subjects.

Those at court learned that while worldly success might initially be perceived to be of greatest importance, the true formula for life is learning from others and teaching others to be successful. Contemporary society measures success by the number of things we possess, accolades and awards received, significant positions attained, or the amount of influence or power we wield. Yet, Jesus Christ, whom we follow and whose birth we continue to celebrate during this Christmas season, came among us as a poor man. He achieved few if any of the marks that today are labels for "success," yet more people follow him and his teaching today than any other religious leader. Why? Jesus was the teacher who taught us the formula for life.

Today we hear how Saint Paul, writing to the Colossians, gives the community a "recipe" for success, not in this world necessarily, but more importantly for eternal life, the goal to which his readers and all of us must daily strive.

In today's reading, Paul lays out in systematic order the qualities, virtues, and characteristics that when knitted together become a fabric, a garment that when worn and used properly becomes our garment that makes us followers of Jesus. First, he says we are God's chosen ones. From the beginning we have been given the privilege of being chosen by God. The message has been given to us; we have been entrusted with a special and magnificent gift. We then have a responsibility to clothe ourselves in this message and to bring it to others. Christ is our teacher and we must continue his work by teaching others, not only in words, but in our actions, attitudes, and in general the way we live our Christian call to holiness.

Because we have been chosen, Paul says we are seen as holy and beloved in God's sight. We are special to God; we are his children. To be seen as special in the eyes of the creator is certainly another great privilege. If God considers us holy, then we must respond and act accordingly. We must be holy people, demonstrating by our actions and our words that we desire to follow the pattern of Christ's life. Jesus clearly gave us a pattern for life, a way to live not only for ourselves but for others.

In order to live a life of holiness, patterned on the life of Jesus, Paul presents us with basic qualities that we must weave into the fabric of our own life. He says we must be people of compassion, kindness, humility, meekness, patience, and to bear with one another. Quite obviously, especially in our fast-paced and self-autonomous society, these are lofty and possibly utopian goals. Yet, if we seek to be holy and follow in the footsteps of Christ, we must do our best to not back away from the challenge that these virtues bring, but charge head on and do what is necessary to make these qualities part of our fabric of life.

Compassion and kindness are lofty goals. One of the basic qualities we seek in others is their ability to demonstrate kindness, but often we ourselves are anything but kind. Rather, we are often "at each other's throats," talking little of kindness or compassion, but rather seeking our own ends. Too often we view others as competitors; too much kindness or compassion toward them will place us at a disadvantage. To be kind and compassionate requires us to go beyond ourselves and our limited purview. We must seek to satisfy the needs of others. Kindness and compassion are not easy characteristics to exemplify; yet they are part and parcel of Paul's formula.

Today humility and meekness are often viewed as signs of weakness. Society tells us we must always appear strong, in control and command of any and all situations. Jesus' teaching in the gospel to sit at the low end of the table and wait to be called up higher (Luke 14:10) is inconsistent with today's message for success. We are always told to put our best foot forward. While we must maximize our potential and use God's gifts wisely to demonstrate to others our talent and potential, it should never be done at the expense of others. When applying for a job or entrance to college or other educational endeavors, our resume must be superior and stand out from others. Still, if we take the time and use our wisdom, this can be done in ways that demonstrate Christian humility. Meekness and humility are not weakness, but rather part of the fabric of holiness to which Paul, through his mentor Jesus Christ, calls us.

Patience is also an important virtue that is part of the formula for life. We have all heard the prayer, "O Lord, grant me patience and give it to me now!" Our society wants things instantly. We want instant gratification and success and the wealth and power that go with it. We want instant resolutions to problems, whether it is some type of significant business negotiation or simply the alleviation of personal pain through medication. We often say our internet connection is too slow and seldom think about the rapidity of our world and our day-by-day movement toward globalization. We do not like to wait for anything. We hate to be in lines, whether it is at the bank, the grocery store, or the queue to purchase something in the store.

Yet, if we think about it, many if not most of the great things in life actually take some time. We cannot rush the seasons; they come each year as the calendar dictates. You cannot rush your favorite recipe; great food takes time to prepare and, therefore, a certain sense of patience. Unless we receive a windfall, fortune, success, and prestige also take time. We do not build relationships overnight, but rather over a long period of time. Clearly, the important things in life are earned by some type of patient endurance.

Paul next asks us to bear with one another and to be forgiving. Too often we hold grudges and will not let the past go — past problems, hurts, or injuries, those we have initiated and those perpetrated against us. We use these events of the past as tools to "hammer" people today for the things of the past. Yet, holding onto a grudge and pain from the past actually holds us back; it slows us down. Past hurts are like a ball and chain shackled to our leg. Unless we cut the chain we will always be hindered in our ability to move forward.

Saint Paul says at the climax of the reading that we must envelop all of these virtues and qualities of his message in love, "which binds everything together in perfect harmony" (v. 14). Love is much more than *eros*, romantic love. It is also *fileo*, the love of brothers and sisters, and the greatest form of love, at least from the perspective of the Greeks, *agape*, the concept of service to others. We must bind our compassion, kindness, humility, meekness, and patience together in love through service to others. If we can do this in the peace of Christ, then the love Paul calls us to manifest will most assuredly reign in our hearts. Paul goes on to say that we have all been called to find this peace for it unites us as one body. We can never be a true community of faith if we do not live in harmony. Christ calls us to be one. As Jesus says in John's gospel, "That they may all be one. As you, Father, are in me and I am in you, may they also be in us, so that the world may believe that you have sent me" (John 17:21).

Paul also calls us to be grateful for all things. Our gratitude to God is obviously paramount and primary. We must demonstrate our gratitude and thanksgiving by leading lives that are consistent with his word and message. We are called to proclaim that thanksgiving in "psalms, hymns, and spiritual songs." Our whole life must be one of thanksgiving, however. We must give thanks for the many ways God blesses us — the people who help us along the path of life, for the opportunities that come our way, and for the talents we possess. We should also be grateful, believe it or not, for the weaknesses we possess and the failures in life as these can help us to learn invaluable lessons including adjusting our actions and thinking when necessary.

Paul in short exhorts the Colossians to learn from Christ, the master teacher and take on his persona. We, too, need to take Jesus seriously; we are called to learn the formula for eternal life, to be the Christ to others. A short prayer, first articulated by Saint Teresa of Avila, the Carmelite mystic and religious reformer of the sixteenth century, illustrates the challenge: Christ has no body on earth but yours — no hands, no feet, but yours. Yours are the eyes with which Christ looks with compassion for the world. Christ has no body on earth but yours.

Having a resume that will give us the desired job, entrance into a more well-respected college, or other life opportunity is fine, even necessary in our world. However, if we do not work equally as hard in learning and seeking the formula or resume for eternal life, then all worldly success will have little value. Jesus says it well, "For what will it profit them if they gain the whole world but forfeit their life?" (Matthew 16:26). Let us take this challenge seriously and learn from Jesus what we need to complete our resume for life. Our efforts will bring success and prosperity today, but more importantly, eternal life tomorrow. Amen.

Christmas 2
Ephesians 1:3-14

The Hidden Gifts Of Christ

One Christmas morning, Dennis, Nancy, and their young son, Eric, were traveling south from San Francisco to their home in Los Angeles. They had spent Christmas Eve with relatives in the Bay Area, but both parents had to work the next day, thus, it was necessary to travel on Christmas. About noon, Dennis and Nancy decided they were hungry so they stopped at a local diner for lunch. Naturally, because it was Christmas, the restaurant was nearly empty and Eric, their young son, was the only child in the restaurant.

As they entered the diner, Eric could be heard screaming with great glee, "Hithere," the two-word expression that he always thought was one. The little boy pounded his hands on the metal chair. He was excited and he wiggled and giggled with great joy. Then Nancy, his mother, saw the source of her son's merriment. On the other side of the restaurant sat a man in a tattered coat who was dirty, greasy, and wore baggy pants with his toes extending out from his worn-out shoes. He was smiling at Eric. "Hi there, little baby. Hi there, big boy. I see you." Dennis and Nancy exchanged looks and said without words, *"What are we to do with this poor devil?"*

Meanwhile, the meal they ordered came, but the man on the other side of the room continued to speak: "Do you know pattycake, little boy? Do you know peekaboo?" Eric continued to laugh and answered with his patented phrase, "Hithere." The whole scene was embarrassing to both Dennis and Nancy, so they decided to quickly pay the check and leave. They both implored heaven, *"Lord, let us get out of here before the man speaks to Eric again."*

However, Eric seemed to have other plans as he reached out both arms in a typical gesture of children that says, "Please, pick me up." Eric began to lunge toward the homeless man with his arms open wide.

The man asked Nancy, "Would you let me hold your baby?" There was no need to answer as Eric almost propelled himself into the man's arms. Suddenly an old and apparently homeless man and a very young baby, in a very real way, consummated their love. Eric laid his tiny head upon the man's ragged shoulder. The man's eyes closed and tears flowed down his cheeks. Both Nancy and Dennis were awestruck. "You take care of this baby," said the man to Nancy.

Somehow she managed to respond, "I will."

The man gave Eric back to his mother and said, "God bless you, ma'am. You have given me a great Christmas gift."

Nancy could say nothing more than a muttered, "Thanks." Now with Eric in her arms she and Dennis walked to the car both saying to God, *"Lord, forgive us, forgive us."*

Eric's mother was petrified and, I suspect most of us would be, too, if our infant child had an encounter with a homeless person. Society, unfortunately, has trained us when we perceive danger to remove ourselves from any encounter with those who stand on the fringes or margins of our society — the homeless, victims of AIDS, immigrants, even the elderly. We feel they have nothing to offer; how can something good come from those who are out of the mainstream? But, Nancy learned one of the great lessons of life and received a special revelation of the goodness of humanity, "through the back door," when she and her son gave a homeless man the only gift he wanted, someone who could give unconditional love.

Today, as the Christmas season continues, a time when society considers gifts given and received, we hear how Jesus, one born on the fringes, a poor and homeless child, brought gifts beyond all measure to our world. We, like the woman, only need to make the first step and Jesus will do the rest.

Saint Paul's thanksgiving to the Ephesians in today's lesson is a presentation of the many ways that Christ showered the Christian community, including those at Ephesus, with blessings, suggesting how this fledgling community might respond in faith. First, the Pauline author speaks of how we have been chosen by the Lord. Obviously, this reality began when God first called Abraham, asking him to move from his native land of Ur to what is now Israel, with the promise that if he was faithful he would become the father of a great nation as numerous as the stars in the sky. Throughout salvation history we know of God's faithfulness, even with the continual unfaithfulness of his people.

The Ephesians, and all of us by extension who have inherited the promise, are God's children by adoption. Made in the image and likeness of God, we were chosen by the creator for a special role in salvation history. What a privilege we have been given by God. But with the privilege comes responsibility in an equally challenging way. Children have significant responsibility to their parents. Thus, we, God's children, have the responsibility to hold up our end of the bargain. This means to be obedient, dutiful, and purposeful in our lives.

Another special blessing, a hidden gift from Jesus, is redemption. Jesus was given a mission by his Father. He was asked to initiate the kingdom of God, but this project continues to require our daily efforts. From our personal perspective, Jesus came to die in a salvific way for us. Jesus, the innocent lamb, was sacrificed for our redemption. The sin of the first Adam is now countered by the supreme obedience of the second. Since we have been ransomed by Jesus' sacrifice, we, as with our adoption as God's children, have a responsibility to repay. We must live as those who are ransomed; we must live in hope. Too often today, especially with the seemingly never-ending troubles, obstacles, and difficulties, the temptation to lose hope is great. But, as they say, "Hope springs eternal." Our status as redeemed people, ransomed at a great price, tells us that even in the darkest hour — personal health issues, financial collapse, divorce, or the death of a family member or friend — we must have the confidence, as the gospel says, to believe that Jesus is a light that no darkness can overcome.

The next special hidden gift of Christ to all of us is forgiveness of sins. The scriptures abound with stories about Jesus' desire to forgive sins. The story of the woman caught in adultery (John 8:1-11) presents the best example. There is no question the woman is guilty; Jesus and the woman never deny it. But Jesus' concentration is on forgiveness, not condemnation. He challenges the women's accusers to cast the first stone, but realizing their own sinfulness, they all drift away, one by one. Jesus then forgives the woman with the admonition, "Go your way, and from now on do not sin again" (John 8:11). The Lord's condemnation falls only on those who openly reject his message. On the other hand, any who sought reconciliation found it in Jesus. One of the few people we know, at least as far as scripture is concerned, who is with God now is the thief on the cross who asked Jesus to remember him. We recall Jesus words, "Truly I tell you, today you will be with me in paradise" (Luke 23:43).

The Pauline author says that Jesus has revealed to us another hidden gift, the mystery of his will. What is Christ's will? Paul tells us it is to gather all things in heaven and on earth under his headship. As a community of faith we form a team, but as with all teams, especially those in athletics, there is need for a leader or coach to guide the whole. For us, of course, the leader, the captain is Jesus. He is a central figure of our faith. As the hub of a wheel is essential to hold together the integrity of the whole unit, so the community of faith is nothing without Christ. Paul wants the Ephesians to know that he is only the messenger; he is not the captain. Jesus is the one who leads us. We, in turn, must be team players. While individual effort is essential in any team endeavor, it is the team that is most important. We must work together if we are to properly build the kingdom.

Another special hidden gift is our inheritance from Christ. This gift is nothing less than life. Following in the footsteps of Jesus, we will find the fullness of life today. Obviously, there is no guarantee that every day will go perfectly. From the fall of Adam, we live in a difficult, problematic, and sinful world. We are all participants in this reality. Yet, following Jesus will give us the fullness of life today. Guided by the light of Christ we will be able to maximize our potential to the fullness of the people we are called to be. More importantly, our inheritance will be, when God calls us home, eternal life. This is the most special of all gifts from Christ. Jesus has promised us we will hear his words: "Come, you that are blessed by my Father, inherit the kingdom prepared for you from the foundation of the world" (Matthew 25:34b).

Lastly, the Pauline author says that the community of faith of which we are members has been marked by the seal of the Holy Spirit. We cannot see the Spirit, but we know, after the first Pentecost, the Spirit entered the world, as Jesus had promised. The presence of the Spirit, sanctifying our world, unites the gifts of Christ and helps us, through our words and actions, to manifest those gifts to others.

The Christmas season is marked by a spirit of giving and receiving. While we spend lots of time and energy in crowded malls, preparing meals, and generally working to bring gifts and joy to others, the greatest gift we received this Christmas is Jesus himself. He brings with him all sorts of hidden gifts. As the homeless man and the little boy's mother each received hidden gifts at Christmas, so too Jesus showers us with gifts beyond our imagination. We have been chosen as God's adopted children. Jesus came to ransom us and to forgive our sins. God's plan to bring the world together in Christ has been revealed to us, and we have become inheritors of life, the fullness of life today and eternal life tomorrow. May we have the courage to respond to Christ's gifts, to maximize our potential and share our gifts, opportunities, and time with others in response to Christ. May the Christian spirit of giving allow us to give freely to others and thus respond to Christ, the giver of all good gifts. Amen.

The Epiphany Of Our Lord
Ephesians 3:1-12

Ambassadors Of The Lord

There is an ancient Christian story that speaks of a fourth wise man, Artaban, in his pursuit of the king of the Jews. As he journeyed with his friends, Caspar, Melchior, and Balthazar, he became separated from them. He never made it to Bethlehem. For many years he sought the Christ Child and in the process had many adventures and assisted many people, including dying beggars and frightened mothers, to whom he gave two of the three great jewels he had originally planned to give to Jesus. He even traveled to Egypt, hearing that Jesus and his parents had gone there, but was again frustrated in his quest. Now, after 33 years of searching he arrived in Jerusalem, hoping at last that he might find the child.

At Passover time, Artaban, now an old man, noted an unusual commotion and inquired about its cause. People answered him, "We are going to the place called Golgotha, just outside the walls of the city, to see two robbers and a man named Jesus of Nazareth, who are being crucified on crosses. The man Jesus calls himself the Son of God, and Pontius Pilate has sent him to be crucified because he claims to be the king of the Jews."

Artaban knew instinctively that this is the king he had been searching for his whole life. Thus, he rushed to the scene. On the way he encountered a young girl being sold into slavery. She saw his royal robes and fell at his feet pleading with him to rescue her. His heart was moved and he gave away the last jewel for her ransom. Just then, darkness fell over the land and the earth shook, and great stones fell into the streets. One of them fell upon Artaban, crushing his head.

As he lay dying in the arms of the girl he had just ransomed, he cried out in a weak voice, "Three and thirty years I looked for thee, Lord, but I have never seen thy face nor ministered to thee!" Then a voice came from heaven, strong and kind, which said, "Inasmuch as you did it to one of the least of my brothers or sisters, you did it to me." Artaban's face grew calm and peaceful. His long journey was ended. He had found his king!

This popular story, taken from the apocrypha of Christian tradition, powerfully presents the Epiphany message. The three magi of whom Saint Matthew speaks in his gospel brought their gifts of gold, frankincense, and myrrh, recognizing Jesus as priest, prophet, and king. Additionally, their presence in Bethlehem demonstrated how Christ was manifest to the nations. In a similar way, Artaban's adventure illustrated another essential idea — that Christ calls us to manifest his glory to all nations. Artaban's goodness and openness to all, even those he did not know, brought the face of Christ, namely the one he sought, to him. Additionally, those to whom he came, the poor and destitute, became Christ to him. Without realizing it, all his life he had been achieving his goal, to see the Christ Child. We, in turn, are challenged to be Christ to others; we must be ambassadors of the Lord.

Saint Paul clearly understood his role as an ambassador of Christ, but he had to learn the lesson "the hard way." The scriptures, both the Acts of the Apostles and the letter to the Galatians, tell us that Paul was a zealous persecutor of "the new way." He was present at and condoned the martyrdom of Stephen (Acts 7:54-60). But God had plans for Paul and directed him to his assigned task as the "apostle to the Gentiles" when he revealed his glory to him on the road to Damascus. Paul was the first and foremost of Christian missionaries. He, in a figurative sense, turned the world upside down by his preaching that this crucified man, Jesus, was Messiah and Lord. He was an especially hard working and dedicated ambassador of the Lord, completing three major missionary journeys around the Eastern Mediterranean world, forming Christian communities, instructing the faithful, and leaving a great legacy in his corpus of letters, which have become the basic foundation for Christian theology.

In today's reading, Paul writes to the Ephesians and reminds them of his special commission from God. As an ambassador of the Lord he has been sent to proclaim Jesus' message of inclusion. He says the mystery of the past, meaning the time before Christ, has now been revealed: "The Gentiles have become fellow heirs, members of the same body, and sharers in the promise in Christ Jesus through the gospel" (Ephesians 3:6). Paul goes on to say that his role as an ambassador means he is a servant of the gospel. While Paul calls himself "the very least of all the saints," due largely one might think from his earlier life, still God's grace was given so he could bring the good news of the boundless riches of Christ to all. Paul's task was to reveal the message of Christ that all were acceptable; no one was to be excluded.

Paul, however, is not simply informing the Ephesians of his role in God's plan; more importantly he is challenging that Christian community to fulfill its responsibility and, like Paul, be ambassadors of the Lord. He says that the church, in Ephesus and more generally God's people everywhere, are to carry forth the message, namely that all are acceptable to God.

Lastly, Paul exhorts his readers not to lose heart. He knows from his own experience that there will be difficult days; the road of being an ambassador of the Lord will not be easy. He says with Christ we can be bold and should have confidence. Thus, he tells his readers not to lose heart but rather to carry forward the mission and the message to others. Jesus' message is universal, thus Paul challenges the Ephesians to do their part, to shoulder the burden and bring Christ to the world.

We, members of the contemporary church, have the same responsibility given by Paul to the Ephesians. In today's world we often hear of people who serve as ambassadors. Most nations have ambassadors, men and women, who are sent to foreign lands to serve as representatives of the ideas, policies, and people of that nation. When heads of state need something from another nation they generally begin that quest by speaking with the ambassador, whose task it is to have the requisite knowledge and to follow the ideas and principles of the nation he or she represents.

Although he did not understand it, Artaban was a great ambassador of Christ. He *thought* he never met Jesus, but realized on death's door that he had been serving the Lord his whole adult life through his consistent, ever faithful, and diligent search for the Christ Child, a search which allowed him to serve many people. Artaban's experience tells us that, while being an ambassador is a necessary element to our common Christian vocation of holiness, we need not fulfill this responsibility in formal ways. In fact, few people will ever have the overt call, as did Saint Paul, to travel far and wide to foreign lands in an effort to bring Christ's message to the world. But this does not in any way negate or remove our responsibility. Being ambassadors of Christ is generally fulfilled in simple, yet profound ways. If we are to bring the message, then in essence we must bring the face of Christ to others as did Artaban.

Being the Christ to others is truly an awesome task. It is not the easy path, but then Jesus never promised that being his followers would be easy. Remember his great challenge:

> *If any want to become my followers, let them deny themselves and take up the cross and follow me. For those who want to save their life will lose it, and those who lose their life for my sake, and for the sake of the gospel, will save it.*   — Mark 8:34b-35

We cannot shy away from this responsibility. There is too much riding on our failure if we do not accept our task to be ambassadors of the Lord. A little story captures our need to be responsible and the ramifications if we fail to answer the call:

One Friday night two rival high school football teams were playing their annual game. One team was, at least on paper, much better than the other. The players were bigger and faster, the team had a better record, and they had supreme confidence. The coach of the underdogs, realizing that he did not have the players to beat the other team, believed his one hope was Calhoun, the fastest halfback in the area.

Toward the end of the fourth quarter, the game was still close; the underdog team was only behind by four points. So the coach called a timeout and brought the team to the sidelines. He gave the players their last instructions. He said, "Men we can win this game, but our only chance is to give the ball to Calhoun." He instructed the quarterback to give the ball to Calhoun who could hopefully score a touchdown and win the game. On first down the quarterback gave the ball to another player who gained little. The coach didn't understand and sent in a player with the words, "Tell the quarterback — give the ball to Calhoun."

On second down the quarterback again gave the ball to another back resulting in no gain. The coach was becoming frustrated and again yelled out onto the field, "You know the plan; give the ball to Calhoun." On third down the quarterback tried a bootleg, but achieved little. Not understanding what was going on, the coach again sent in a player and told him, "We have one last chance; the play is to give the ball to Calhoun." On fourth down the quarterback went back to pass and was sacked. With that time ran out and the game was over.

The coach, frustrated beyond all belief, ran to the quarterback and asked him, "You knew the plan; why didn't you give the ball to Calhoun?"

The young quarterback answered, "Coach, each time we called the play, but Calhoun didn't want the ball." The message is clear; we must take our responsibility seriously. When God or others "call our number" we must take the ball and run with it.

How does one manifest being an ambassador of the Lord, being the Christ to others? First, we must be the person God calls us to be. If our vocation is marriage and family, then we should be the best spouse, parent, and worker we can be. If called to the single life, we might have more time to directly assist others and to be a more overt ambassador. Young people must fulfill their roles, assisting with family duties and chores, maximizing their efforts in the classroom, showing their peers the Christian way to resolve problems regardless of what contemporary society might suggest is the "quick fix" to what ails us personally or communally.

Being ambassadors is not a nine-to-five job. We must be Christians 24 hours a day seven days a week. A little story captures this challenge. One day a reporter was interviewing a well-respected man of the community. He asked him, "What do you do?"

The answer came back almost immediately, "I am a Christian."

"No," said the reporter, "you do not understand what I mean. What keeps you busy; what do you do every day?"

Again, the man responded, "I told you I am a Christian." Somewhat frustrated, the reporter for the third time asked, "No, sir, you do not understand my question. What do you do for a living; how do you occupy your time? What is your livelihood?"

The man once again answered, "I told you I am a Christian 24 hours a day seven days a week. But to pay the bills I own a furniture store."

Our role as ambassadors is part and parcel of our lives as Christians. Let us realize that like Artaban we may not *think* that our lives make a difference, but we are all players in God's magnificent plan of salvation history. Let us do our share to build the kingdom of God in our world. Let us be ambassadors of the Lord, today and to life eternal. Amen.

**The Baptism Of Our Lord
Epiphany 1
Ordinary Time 1
Acts 8:14-17**

Responsibility Comes With Privilege

Once upon a time there was a good king who ruled wisely and well over his people, who loved him very much. This king had four beautiful daughters who were all well respected by the people. One day he called them together and told them, "I am going to a far-off monastery to spend time in prayer with God. Therefore, I am leaving you in charge of the kingdom." While all the girls, one after the other, told their father not to leave, he insisted that it was necessary. Before he left on his journey, however, he gave each one a small gift, one single grain of rice. Then, after hugging and kissing his daughters, he set off on his journey.

Each of the daughters used the gift in different ways. The eldest thought the gift was special and wanted to display it. She went to her room, tied a long, golden thread around the grain of rice and placed it in a beautiful crystal box on her bureau. She could see it each day and it reminded her of her father, the king. The second daughter also believed the gift to be important. She placed her grain of rice in a wooden box and put it in a secure place under her bed. The third daughter, who was very pragmatic, looked at the grain of rice and thought, "What good is one grain of rice?" She simply discarded it. The youngest daughter took the grain of rice to her room and began to ponder what the significance of her father's gift was. She thought about it for weeks, then a month. After nearly a year had passed, she believed she understood the meaning of the gift.

Months turned into years and the four daughters ruled their father's kingdom. Then one day the king returned with a sparkle in his eye and a certain illumination in his face that he gained from years of prayer. After greeting each one of his daughters he asked to see the gifts that he had given to them. The eldest daughter retrieved the crystal box containing the grain of rice on the golden thread. The king accepted the crystal box and the grain of rice saying, "Thank you." Similarly, the king accepted the wooden box from the second daughter, saying to her, "Thank you." The third daughter rushed into the kitchen, found a grain of rice, and brought it back to her father who accepted it, again saying, "Thank you."

Then the youngest daughter came forward. She explained to her father that she had thought long and hard about the meaning of the gift and finally realized that it was a seed. So she planted it. Soon it grew and from it she harvested other seeds which she again planted. This continued over many seasons. She said to her father, "Father, look at the enormous crop of rice that we now have. It is enough to feed our entire nation."

Stepping before his daughter, the king took off his golden crown and placed it on her head. "You have learned the meaning of how to rule," he said softly. From that day on the youngest daughter ruled the kingdom wisely and well.

The story of the king and his four daughters demonstrates that privilege and responsibility come together; they cannot be separated. Each of the women received the same privilege, the honor of ruling their father's kingdom. The first three did not understand the responsibility that came with the privilege. The youngest, however, after contemplating the significance of her father's gift, realized the need to be responsible. Thus, she was the one chosen to succeed her father.

Today we close the Christmas season by celebrating the Baptism of our Lord. We are reminded not only of the Lord's baptism, as we hear described by all the synoptic evangelists, but possibly more importantly our own baptism. This sacrament brought us great privileges but significant responsibility is ours as well.

The Acts of the Apostles, from which our lesson is taken today, is really two books in one. Often referred to as the "fifth gospel," due to its probable authorship by Saint Luke, and its content, Acts presents two separate but important stories. In the early chapters we hear about the nascent Christian church, the formation of the community of faith, and some of the early struggles of these people, our ancestors in the faith. The latter portion of Acts chronicles the conversion of Saint Paul and then provides a detailed description of his three missionary journeys, for which he is often called the "apostle to the Gentiles."

The apostles and their close followers realized that they were privileged people. To walk in the footsteps of Jesus and to be his representatives on earth were indeed significant privileges. Persecution notwithstanding, these early Christians fearlessly and with great zeal and persistence carried on the work of their master amongst the people of their day and locale. Peter and John, two of the inner circle, realized that the privilege they had received in being apostles required that they take seriously their responsibilities.

Thus, as we hear in the reading, they brought the Holy Spirit, the same gift they had received at Pentecost to the people of Samaria. Recall that these people were the remnant of the so-called "ten lost tribes of Israel," overrun by the Assyrians and lost to history in 722 BCE. The apostles realized that Jesus' message of inclusivity went to all, even the long-despised Samaritans. Therefore, they unhesitatingly go to their natural enemy, realizing that they have a responsibility to carry forth the message of Christ to all people. Thus, they share the great gift that Jesus sent, the Holy Spirit, with others. Like the youngest daughter in the story, they understood that responsibility came with the privilege of carrying the message of Christ. Fortunately, through the efforts of people like the original apostles, Saint Paul, and many other brave men and women of that early Christian community, the message has been preached throughout the world. The Christian community has taken its responsibility seriously.

Baptism, the common denominator for all Christians, is a rare privilege. We have the privilege of being adopted children of God. Too often we brush over this significant prize of being children of God. However, only a few moments of reflection will show us how great a privilege God has bestowed upon all of us. We have the privilege of the church and all the many things it brings us — the sacraments, the word of God, the community of faith, fellowship, and assistance. We have each other as our friends, brothers, and sisters in the Lord, to celebrate our triumphs and to mourn our losses.

This great privilege of being a baptized Christian, however, has many responsibilities that come with it. Like Peter, John, and the other first-century Christians, we, the contemporary baptized, have the responsibility to carry forth the message of Christ to others. We are to preach the good news, both in formal and informal ways. We can teach an academic class, go door-to-door to evangelize, or even stand on a street corner and preach the message of Jesus. Clearly, these can be very effective methods, but they are by no means the only ones. In fact, meeting our baptismal commitment, fulfilling our responsibilities as Christians, happens each and every day of our lives in ways that are often routine, ordinary, and even seemingly mundane.

For example, simply walking along the street and sharing with a passerby a friendly smile and a cheery, "Good morning," is preaching the goodness of God to others. We can preach Christ's message of love, care, and peace through a gentle disposition, random acts of kindness, assisting those in need, or going out of our way to help someone, especially one whom we do not know. Parents and others in positions of authority carry out their baptismal commitment by being responsible for those whom God has given to them — children, grandchildren, fellow employees, and fellow travelers along the road of faith.

We have responsibilities to our places of work, the neighborhoods where we reside, and the community we call home, both on local and even national levels. Young people demonstrate their baptismal commitment by being responsible to their school work and classmates, their parents, and after school jobs. They show responsibility by avoiding the many pitfalls into which they are pressured: violence, drinking, sex, and drugs. In short, the privilege of being a baptized person necessitates we take seriously our Christian responsibilities.

Our fast-paced and highly technological world challenges us in many ways. Self-autonomy, desire for personal advancement, and the need to always shine above others often does not allow us to spend the time that is necessary to meet our responsibilities. Additionally, we fall victim to apathy, indifferentism, laziness, and even a sense of fatalism. We say, "Why should I get involved? Things will be the same with or without my effort." It is easy to take this road because it is well-traveled and quite popular, but for the Christian it is a dead-end street. We must accept the reality that responsibility is part and parcel of our lives as baptized Christians. All great privileges bring with them a sense of responsibility. We readily and with great joy accept the former, but only grudgingly, at times, fulfill the latter.

While the road will not be easy, nor the path straight, we must nevertheless push forward with vigor and persistence the Christian agenda that calls us to be responsible people, to be countercultural in a world that often does not understand or value the things we do or the beliefs we profess. Let us understand our responsibilities to family, neighbor, community of faith, and most especially to God. Let us as they say, "Take the ball and run with it," and sprint toward the goal, which is not a touchdown, but more importantly eternal life. Amen.

**Epiphany 2
Ordinary Time 2
1 Corinthians 12:1-11**

Strength Through Diversity

Recently on a British Airways flight from Johannesburg, South Africa, a middle-aged and apparently quite wealthy South African woman found herself sitting next to a black man. As the passengers were filing in and taking their seats she called a member of the cabin crew to ask about her seating. "What seems to be the matter, madam?" asked the attendant.
"Can't you see?" the woman responded. "You have assigned me a seat next to a *kaffir* (a pejorative word referring to a native black African). I cannot possibly sit next to this disgusting human being. Please find me another seat as soon as possible!"
The cabin attendant, hearing the words and observing the commotion that was clearly stirring among other passengers, commented, "Please calm down, madam. The flight is very full today but I will do what I can. I will go and check on availability of seats in business or first classes."
Meanwhile the woman, with a scowl on her face, looked at the black man beside her, who was outraged, not to mention many of the surrounding passengers. A few minutes later the attendant returned with good news that she delivered to the woman, who continued to look at her fellow passengers with a smug and self-satisfied grin. The flight attendant told the woman, "Madame, unfortunately, as I suspected economy is full. I have spoken to the cabin services director and business class is also full. However, we do have one seat in first class."
Before the woman had a chance to answer, the flight attendant continued, "It is most extraordinary to make this kind of upgrade;

I needed to receive special permission from the captain. But, given the circumstances, the captain felt that it was outrageous that someone be forced to sit next to such an obnoxious person." With that the flight attendant turned to the black man sitting next to the woman and said, "So if you would like to gather your things, sir, I have your seat ready for you." At that point, the surrounding passengers stood and gave a standing ovation as the black man walked triumphantly into first class.

This true event presents us with many lessons. Most obviously we learn of the reality of prejudice and intolerance in our world. The story also shows how one can learn a significant lesson from those with greater wisdom that such prejudicial attitudes do not gain us anything, but rather can shame us into realizing the callous nature of our attitudes. Somewhat hidden, but nonetheless present, the story also tells us of the great value diversity can bring, especially with the knowledge that all things have one source, namely God, and we are to work toward one common end, the building of God's kingdom. Although our methods will be different, we must use the gifts we possess and our varied cultures and racial ethnicities to assist others toward the common goal of life eternal. Openness to what is new and different is key to appreciating the power, goodness, and strength that can come from diversity.

Saint Paul addresses the issue of diversity in today's reading by describing the various gifts we have received, all of which have one common source, the Holy Spirit. First, Paul speaks of the necessity of the Spirit in our lives. He writes that we can only address Jesus as Lord by the inspiration of the Spirit. We are not autonomous operators; God is here to inspire and encourage us. God does not force us to do anything, but the inspiration is given to lead us in the proper direction — the one and only path that leads back to God. Thus, the Spirit is necessary to continue toward God. Paul also says that if we have the Spirit, we cannot speak ill of God. Living in the power and presence of God has its positive effects on us. We cannot go astray with God, but there are many lessons we need to learn in order to achieve this result.

The apostle then enumerates the many gifts of the Spirit. Each is unique and special; each is given, Paul says, as the Spirit chooses.

Each gift is different and must be used in a collective sense with others in building the kingdom of God. It is through this diversity of gifts that we find our source of sustenance. We need all the gifts, but none of us has them all. Thus, we need to appreciate the diversity, the differences, and the strength that we gain through sharing with one another. If all the world's people had the same gifts, human society would never achieve its potential. As Paul says, the manifestations of the Spirit's gifts are given for the common good.

We have all experienced the plethora of the Spirit's gifts, in our lives and the lives of those we know, love, and with whom we regularly associate. Some are given great wisdom; some are given significant knowledge. We know that these two gifts are very different, but both are necessary to build the kingdom. We need a certain amount of knowledge — that is people who are smart — but we definitely need people who know how to apply that knowledge, those with wisdom to apply facts and information.

Paul continues by describing many gifts, each given by the Spirit, each different and unique. Whether it is faith, healing, being a worker of miracles, prophecy, languages, or one who interprets languages, the gift is part of the breath of God's goodness. These gifts, together with knowledge and wisdom, show the diversity of our talents. All are important; all are necessary. While we might live without one of the gifts in our personal lives, our world would be somewhat less without any of them. We would all be deprived of something very special.

We have all heard the expression "Diversity is the spice of life." I think we can all verify the reality of this statement. Picture a world where all people looked, spoke, acted, and thought alike. It would be like entering a shoe store and finding only one style or going to a car dealership that offered only one make or model of automobile or finding only one brand of cereal or bread in the grocery store. Simply put, life would be boring and certainly less than satisfying. Yet, as is evidenced by the story of the passengers on the plane and, too often unfortunately in the world around us, indeed in our own lives at times, we reject diversity. We are selective.

Everyone makes choices; nobody likes everyone or everything. The rejection of diversity is not that we don't acknowledge differences in talents, ideas, ethnic or national backgrounds, or possess varied religious or political persuasions. Rather when we reject diversity we openly reject that which is different around us. Most of the time, our rejection of diversity is rather subtle. We choose not to associate with certain people, either individuals or collective groups. There are times we never consider another person's idea, way of doing things, or attitude if it differs from ones we hold. We isolate ourselves from what we do not like or simply do not wish to deal with. Most probably we don't even realize that we are rejecting diversity. Rather, we say to ourselves, "I simply have different ideas than others."

Too often, however, society and individuals openly reject diversity, even in a hostile way. That was certainly the case with the woman on the plane. We may not make a scene as did the woman, but in our minds and actions we are as closed as she was toward the black man. Such attitudes stunt our growth. Sometimes we are fortunate, like the woman, to be shocked or even embarrassed into understanding the problematic reality of our attitude. However, too often we do not learn and thus we continue down the path that leads nowhere. We miss out on many opportunities of life.

The destructive force of a world without diversity has, unfortunately, been repeated too often in history. The suppression of native people in the New World and the perceived need to have one and only one culture deprived the world of a few significant civilizations, such as the Aztec, Mayan, and Inca native people in Mexico and South America. Religious wars in Europe, the infamous crusades of medieval times, and many wars between rival Christian factions were fought basically because people were not open to varied understandings of God. Certainly such actions were an overt denial of Jesus' message of inclusivity. Intolerance in ways of thinking, politically and socially, generated the Soviet State's control of the "Iron Curtain" countries after World War II. Rejection of the Jews as a race, culture, and religion led directly to the Holocaust. These historical events stunted the world's ability to grow for a time. We were all the losers.

We need to root out the attitude of exclusivity, the idea that some people, ideas, opinions, and attitudes are acceptable while others are not. We may not agree with certain ways of doing things, but we cannot dismiss them out of hand. Such behavior not only contradicts the message of Paul and his diversity of spiritual gifts for the common good, but it betrays the whole life of Jesus, the head and guide of our faith. Therefore, let us learn a lesson today of the need to appreciate variations in our world. Let us truly believe that strength comes through diversity. As we continue to walk as one people, rejoicing in our different talents, gifts, ideas, let us do so in imitation of Jesus, our brother, friend, and Lord. Amen.

**Epiphany 3
Ordinary Time 3
1 Corinthians 12:12-31a**

Teammates In Building The Kingdom

"Outlined against a blue-gray October sky, the Four Horsemen rode again. In dramatic lore they are known as pestilence, famine, destruction, and death. These are only aliases. There real names are Studehler, Miller, Crowley, and Layden." Grantland Rice, a well-known sports columnist in the first half of the twentieth century, wrote those memorable words in October 1927 after attending a classic gridiron struggle between Army and Notre Dame, played at the Polo Grounds in New York. With these words a legend was started, for Notre Dame football, the team's immortal coach Knute Rockne and, that day especially, for the Four Horsemen of Notre Dame.

Who were the Four Horsemen? Elmer Layden, Harry Studehler, Jim Crowley, and Don Miller were the talented offensive backfield for the Notre Dame football team in the late 1920s. There is no doubt that they were great players. Football fans then and now remember their names and their exploits on the gridiron. All four have been enshrined in the College Football Hall of Fame.

Most people know, however, that there are eleven players on a football team. What about the other seven? Who were they; what did they do? History knows them as the "Seven Mules." Few if anyone remembers their names. Only one of them, a fellow named "Rip" Miller, is a member of the College Football Hall of Fame. Still, I am certain that the Four Horsemen knew them. In fact, the same Grantland Rice who immortalized the horsemen said that this talented backfield attributed all their success to the mules. They were the ones who stood in front, did the blocking, ran interference, and paved a way for the two halfbacks, the fullback, and quarterback to run the plays, score touchdowns, and bring victory to Notre Dame.

The Four Horsemen and the Seven Mules were a team. They knew that they needed each other. Without the mules the horsemen probably would have been an ordinary college football backfield. But the combination of the mules and the horsemen, working as a team, brought greatness, fame, and legend to Miller, Layden, Crowley, Studehler, and to Notre Dame football, as well.

The story of the fabled Four Horsemen of Notre Dame and the unheralded "seven mules," is a good illustration of how people need to work together to accomplish great goals. We are not solo operators in the world; we need each other. While we may be different and possess varied talents, in this case some to run with the ball and others to block and run interference, all are needed to achieve the desired common end. In a similar way, Saint Paul uses the famous image of the body to demonstrate that while we are different in many ways, possessive of various gifts and talents, we must be united as the body of Christ in our common effort to build the kingdom of God in our world.

Paul begins his famous analogy by describing the power of baptism in unifying the body of Christ. He says that our baptism in the Spirit unites us, whether Jews or Greek, slave or free. Thus, Paul touches on both of the critical bases: sacred and secular. Not only are the Jews, those who were the first converts to Christianity, part of the body, but also the Greeks, that is the Gentiles. Jesus' message of salvation goes out to all. He goes on to say slaves as well as free men and women are part of the body. Here Paul suggests that status in the world is of little or no consequence to Christ. Baptism is the great leveler, the right that is common to all. His message says that no one is more or less important in Jesus' eyes.

Paul's analogy of membership to the body continues by speaking of the contributions of hands and feet, eyes and ears. In both cases each part of the body is of significant value. One part cannot say of the other it is not part of the body or unimportant. All parts are members, all parts are important. He goes on to say that each part is essential. If the body were all an eye or an ear then other senses, such as smell and touch, would be lost. Indeed, Paul says that the parts that seem weaker are actually indispensable. Those with less honor are clothed with greater honor. God has arranged to give greater honor to those inferior members so that there will be no dissension.

God desires the body of Christ to work together. If it is truly united then when one part suffers the whole body suffers; when one member is honored the whole body rejoices. The body, therefore, must live, love, and cry together. The body is one; its strength comes through unity.

Paul concludes his analogy by providing examples of how the parts of the body are manifest. He mentions apostles, prophets, teachers as some of the many specific vocations of the body. Then he describes the many gifts, such as healing, assistance, forms of leadership, and tongues or languages. No one person possesses all of these gifts and, thus, there is a need to work together to maximize the potential of the body. Again, Paul stresses the need for unity.

Paul's analogy of the body working together clearly presents the message that we must be a team, working with Jesus, our leader and guide. Saint Augustine in his great work, *The City of God*, wrote that we are citizens of two worlds, human society and the church. In each of these domains it is necessary to be a team, to work on a united front. We must, however, realize that unity does not mean uniformity. We don't all march to the same drummer; we have various likes and dislikes, different ways of operation. Thus, our methods and ideas will vary, which is actually helpful to the progress of the body. We can and must approach situations and problems with various solutions. What is essential, however, is to remain on the same page with respect to the goal. There are many ways to skin a cat; achieving the desired end is essential. Thus, the body can use all its members to gain its goal, not only a few who are prominent, influential, or noteworthy.

But what is our goal? We are called to build the kingdom of God in our world. In essence we are to build a more compassionate, peaceful, and just world. We have been commissioned through baptism to do our share to complete the master's work. Jesus' work in our world is multidimensional but has been succinctly described by Father Basil Anthony Moreau, founder of the Congregation of Holy Cross, who wrote that our mission is, "to make God known, loved, and served."

We can carry out this mission in our world in many ways. We have varied locations, occupations, and gifts. We need doctors, attorneys, teachers, office workers, police and fire personnel, engineers, and a host of other peoples to make civil society one that functions properly. Each contributes in his or her individual and specific way. However, we must keep our eyes focused on the goal, to make God known, loved, and served.

Unfortunately, too many divisions exist in our world. We are not running the race together as a team, but rather, seem to be individual athletes in competition. This competition between groups and individuals is strong and even becomes counterproductive toward the achievement of the common goal. The body, therefore, is fighting against itself. Thus, society is not moving sufficiently toward its proper end. On the contrary, there is much evidence we are moving increasingly away from our common goal.

Such evidence is clear in the North-South economic division of our world that continues to grow, separating nations and people. Paul suggests that if the body of Christ must suffer, it must do so together. Unfortunately, this is not the reality. The vast majority of the world suffers and lives in darkness. The manifestations of this reality are many and widespread. Poverty, disease, ignorance, injustice, and violence are only some of the many significant ways the world suffers. We do not care sufficiently for our weaker members, as Paul suggests. Rather we place them on the margins of society, unseen and unheard. The majority feels better when such "problematic" individuals are kept out of mind and sight. Again, we contradict the body of Christ in our actions. On the other hand, a limited few exult. These possess not only what they need but in many cases have superabundance. While it is true that Jesus said, "The poor you will always have with you," we cannot use this as an excuse to ignore the inequalities in our world.

What is even sadder is that the majority of the world suffers and a few exult due in large measure to personal choice. Nations and individuals make decisions that create the world in which we live. It is not simply the progress of history that creates poverty and wealth. No, human society has chosen this route.

The lack of teamwork in human society is, unfortunately, replicated in our church. Rather than working together as a team, we are far too divided. Often, it seems, we are actually working against each other. Distinctions that divide communities of faith seem more important than ideas that unite us. Again, personal choice is, in large measure, the reason for this situation.

Solutions to this situation can and must be found. In society we can create a more compassionate and just world by focusing more on others and less on ourselves. While we cannot change a societal attitude on a systemic level overnight, we can and must change our own attitude. As the expression goes, "Think globally but act locally." If we can begin to move more toward an attitude of community and push away from individualism in our personal lives and that of society, we will have at least made a good start. In our churches we must move toward greater ecumenical and even interfaith dialogue. Again, we must begin with ourselves realizing that men and women of faith worldwide have good intentions. Thus, to concentrate on what is common and constructive rather than that which is divisive will get us started in the proper direction.

Saint Paul's image of the body of Christ, many members working together, sharing our joys and sorrows, is our goal. However, society and the church are far from this lofty summit. Let our goal be to work toward making the body one in our society. Let us work together as a team, like the Four Horsemen and the seven mules. Jesus' prayer to his Father can light our way: "That they may all be one. As you, Father, are in me and I am in you, may they also be in us, so that the world may believe that you have sent me" (John 17:21). Let us profess and believe the same. Amen.

Epiphany 4
Ordinary Time 4
1 Corinthians 13:1-13

Love — The Basic Christian Call

During the 56 years of his life, Adolf Hitler did incredible harm and was responsible for the death of millions of people. Yet in all of the horror that he unleashed, there were pinpoints of light and nobility. One German soldier, Private Joseph Schultz, was one of those pinpoints.

Schultz was sent to Yugoslavia shortly after the Germans invaded that country. He was a loyal, young, German soldier on patrol. One day the sergeant called out eight names, his among them. They thought they were going on a routine patrol. As they hitched up their rifles, they came over a hill, still not knowing what their mission was. There they encountered eight Yugoslavians, standing on the brow of a hill, five men and three women. It was only when they were about fifty feet away from them, when any marksman could shoot out the eye of a pheasant, that the soldiers realized what their mission was.

The soldiers were lined up. The sergeant barked out, "Ready!" and they lifted their rifles. "Aim," and the soldiers got their sights set. Then suddenly in the silence that prevailed there was the thud of a rifle butt against the ground. The sergeant, the seven other soldiers, and those eight Yugoslavians stopped and looked. Private Joseph Schultz walked toward the Yugoslavians. His sergeant called after him and ordered him to come back, but he pretended not to hear him. Instead, Schultz walked fifty feet to the mound of the hill and he joined hands with the eight Yugoslavians. There was a moment of silence, and then the sergeant yelled, "Fire!" Private Schultz died that day, his blood mingled with those of the innocent men and women. Found on his body was an excerpt from Saint Paul: "[Love] bears all things, believes all things, hopes all things, endures all things" (1 Corinthians 13:7).

This true story from World War II demonstrates the concept of love as articulated by Saint Paul in his famous passage from 1 Corinthians. The many manifestations of love are brought together by Paul who understood this powerful emotion through his imitation of Jesus and the latter's commandment of love. We are similarly called to love without reservation.

Saint Paul begins his teaching by describing the many ways love excels all other virtues. He says one may be able to speak with great force and angelic quality, but if there is no love behind the words, the person is a noisy gong or clanging symbol. Clearly, the intent, the reason one speaks is of great importance for Paul. One must speak with the proper intent — never to injure, but always to demonstrate love. This does not mean, at times, that hard words are not necessary. Tough love may demand words that others do not want to hear; to act in any other way would not be a demonstration of love.

The apostle then speaks of the power of love over prophecy. We may have been given the gift to understand great mysteries and the opportunity to proclaim them to others, but without love we are not utilizing the gift in an appropriate manner. Knowledge is given to aid others and to build the kingdom of God. If, however, we do not have love in our use of this knowledge it is easy to misuse it or to utilize it in inappropriate ways. It will not be used to build the kingdom.

Again, Paul says we may have faith so strong we can move mountains, yet without love we have nothing. Faith in God mandates that we have great love; faith without love cannot be faith in God, for God is love.

Lastly, Paul says if we give all we have away and give our bodies over for others to use in some way but do not possess love we gain nothing. There is no activity of charity or compassion that can be rightly done without love. We may give but if there is no love behind our gift, then most probably we are giving only to be noticed by others, not for the appropriate reasons.

Thus, Paul provides ample evidence to the reality that love is the basic Christian virtue. It is the foundation upon which all is built; it is the root from which all of Christianity blossoms. Love is absolutely essential if we are to live the Christian life as Jesus outlined it in his words and deeds. While Paul could not have read any of the gospels, he seemed to know a great deal about Jesus, including his new commandment of love. Jesus expresses it powerfully.

> *I give you a new commandment, that you love one another. Just as I have loved you, you also should love one another. By this everyone will know that you are my disciples, if you have love for one another.*
> — John 13:34-35

Paul's idea that love is the base of Christianity is clear, but how can we know we actually love as Jesus commanded? The apostle helps us answer this question by providing an important list of qualities present in one who loves. First, he says love is patient. We know patience is a virtue in short supply these days. The humorous little prayer demonstrates our difficulty with patience: "O, Lord, grant me patience and give it to me now!" We don't want to wait for anything these days, in our world and in our personal lives, both of which mandate instant answers and results. We are all impatient, especially when we have no control over responses or results. Paul suggests if we truly love we will demonstrate patience.

Next, he says love is kind. Often impatience leads to a very unkind attitude; we become angry quite readily. The way we approach people and situations is too often far less than kind. We are adversarial; we are right and others are wrong. We somehow believe if we are too kind we demonstrate weakness and others will take advantage of us. Yet, Paul suggests we are not people of love if we cannot demonstrate kindness to our brothers and sisters.

The apostle continues by saying love is never envious or boastful. There are certainly major problems in our society today. We are always trying to impress people with who we are or the things we do. We observe this in many professional athletes, television and movie stars, and politicians. But even more Paul is suggesting that a boastful or envious attitude will destroy relationships. True love for another cannot allow us to be envious of who others are or what they do. We are told by Paul that love is never resentful. If we are envious we are often resentful of what others have been given. We desire their power, wealth, prestige, or some combination of these three. We cannot "lord it over others" simply because circumstance or situation has placed us above others on the corporate or social ladders. True love is incompatible with attitudes that differentiate between peoples or place one person ahead or behind another.

Paul concludes his discussion of love's qualities by providing a list of attributes that demonstrate the positive nature and hopefulness of love. He says love bears through any hardship. We know love is greatly tested when problems and the vicissitudes of life come our way. The person of true love can look down the road and bear through to the end. This is possible because people who love can believe all things are possible. With love, meaning with God, all things truly are possible. We can hope in all things because with love hope is possible. As a popular expression goes, "Hope springs eternal." Love will endure to the end.

Yes, Paul believes love is eternal. While prophecies end through their fulfillment, tongues will fall into disuse, and even knowledge will be lost over time, love will endure. Prophecy, knowledge, and all other ideas are only found in part, but love is eternal. Love is the fulfillment of our life. Paul expresses this idea by seeing love as the adult response to life. In the end, he summarizes his teaching by saying, of all the great virtues of faith, hope, and love, the greatest and, therefore, the base of the Christian life is love.

How can we manifest this great love of God? Joan Baez, the famous folk singer of the 1960s, sang a song titled "Love Is Just A Four Letter Word." The lyrics of the song express the idea that because love is a short word of only four letters it might be thought to be a simple concept. We know, however, that this base virtue of the Christian life is anything but simple. Its manifestations are many. As Private Schultz understood by his heroic actions, love never delights in evil, but rather rejoices in the truth.

The Greeks, a wise and highly sophisticated ancient civilization, understood the complexity of love. Their language uses three words to express the one we have in English. The concept of *eros* speaks of specialized romantic love. Obviously this is an integral element of love where men and women demonstrate their total commitment to each other in marriage. All the qualities of which Paul speaks must clearly be put into a relationship of *eros*. Unfortunately, today we often see the consequences when one or both parties in such a relationship cannot fulfill the qualities and characteristics of which Paul writes.

The Greeks used the word *phileo* to describe brotherly and sisterly love. We have many relationships with members of our family, good friends, colleagues and associates at work, as well as neighbors in our city or town. We must show love for them as well. We cannot like all people; we will only choose to associate for social recreation with a limited group. Others, let us face reality, we might choose to avoid for a whole host of reasons, some of which might be appropriate, but others not very sound. Yet, we are called to demonstrate love to all. In essence we are called to respect people, to never seek our advantage over them, nor denigrate their person or the ideas they express simply because we do not agree. Love calls us to show this common respect.

Lastly, the Greeks use the word *agape* to express their highest form of love — service to one another. While Paul's exhortation on love, on initial examination, does not seem to speak of service, yet all of these qualities are endemic to it. Service requires us to go out of our way, beyond our immediate purview to meet the needs of some of our brothers and sisters. In such endeavors we must show patience and kindness. We must never be boastful or arrogant, placing ourselves above others. We have all heard the expression, "If not by the grace of God, there go I." Our Christian commitment to love calls us to serve others. We must never shirk this most important responsibility.

The manifestations of love are many. Few of us will ever be tested to love as was Private Schultz. His faith constitution was obviously strong, and he made his decision to stand with the Yugoslavians as an act of love. Still, we are challenged on a daily basis to show love, to manifest in our lives with spouses, friends, and associates, and God's people more generally the special qualities of love that Paul describes today. Let us take some time to look into our hearts and ask, "How have we loved today? What more do we need to do?" When we find the answers, let us have the courage as did Private Schultz, Saint Paul, and Jesus of Nazareth and manifest love to others in all that we say and do. If we can, our reward in heaven will be great. Amen.

**Epiphany 5
Ordinary Time 5
1 Corinthians 15:1-11**

The Great Sacrifice Of Love

In the fifteenth century, a rural village in Germany was home to a family with eighteen children. The family was poor, but despite the difficulty of making ends meet, two brothers in the family still held a dream, namely to pursue their talent as artists. With the financial situation bleak the two boys came up with their own solution to the problem. They agreed to toss a coin with the loser going to the local mines to work so he could support the other while he attended art school. When the first was finished with his training, he would support the education of the other, either by sale of his art works or by going to the mines himself. Thus, one brother went off to the dangerous mines while the other went to the art academy. After four years, the young artist returned triumphantly to a homecoming dinner. The artist rose from the table to drink a toast to his beloved brother for his years of sacrifice. He said, "Now Albert, it is your turn to go to the academy and pursue your dream; I will support you."

Albert sat at the table and tears began to flow down his cheeks. He began to repeat, "No, no, no." Finally Albert rose, wiped the tears from his face and holding his hands out in front of him said softly, "No, brother, it is too late for me to go. Look at what four years in the mines have done to my hands. The bones in every finger have been crushed at least once, and I suffer from arthritis so badly that I cannot even hold a wine glass properly to return your toast, much less make lines on a canvas with pen or brush. No, brother, for me it is too late."

Then, one day to pay homage to his brother who had sacrificed his life dream for him, the great artist, Albrecht Dürer, painstakingly drew his brother's hands with palms together and crooked fingers pointed skyward. He called his powerful painting simply *Hands*, but the entire world almost immediately opened its heart to the masterpiece and renamed his great work and tribute of love, *The Praying Hands*.

The story of the great sacrifice of Albert Dürer for his brother is truly inspiring. After hearing his story, whenever one sees Albrecht Dürer's masterpiece, *The Praying Hands*, it is impossible to not associate this work of art with the sacrifice of love it represents. In today's lesson from 1 Corinthians, Saint Paul describes the earliest account of the greatest act of sacrificial love the world has ever witnessed, the Paschal mystery — the passion, death, and resurrection of Jesus Christ. Jesus came to our world in obedience to his Father's will, becoming human in all ways, save sin, and willingly gave his life so we would have the possibility of life eternal. Not only does Paul describe the great sacrifice of Jesus' love for us, he also explains how he responded to this love through his energetic and unceasing missionary activity. Paul's words must challenge us to ask how we can respond in a similar way to the sacrificial love Jesus has shown us.

Saint Paul's encounter with Jesus on the road to Damascus and the long period of preparation (scholars dispute whether it was fourteen or seventeen years) after his conversion for his mission, filled him with the tradition of Jesus. Thus, he wants to educate the Corinthians, a people he knew very well as evidenced by his letters to the community and his residence in the city for a considerable amount of time. He explains to them the significance of the extraordinary sacrifice of love that Jesus performed for us. First Corinthians is the earliest source for these sacred Christian traditions. In 11:23-26, Paul gives the first account of the institution of the Eucharist, one of the basic and common rites in our Christian tradition.

In today's lesson Paul describes the Paschal mystery. He says the great traditions of Jesus were foretold in the scriptures. Jesus is the fulfillment of God's promise. It is through the promise and its fulfillment that the Corinthians and all others will be saved. Thus, it is essential that the community believe in Paul's message for it is the missive of life.

Paul then articulates specifically the great events of our salvation. First, he says that Jesus died. Jesus truly suffered and experienced death for the remission of our sins. But the tradition of Jesus' death and burial is followed by the elation that he was raised and appeared to the apostles and even later to Paul and many other disciples. This great sacrifice of God's love demonstrated the length and breadth of what God was willing to do for us. As Albert Dürer went to the mines so his brother could attend art school, and in the process sacrificed his own opportunity for greatness and personal fulfillment, so Jesus, the Son of God, fulfilled his Father's will and sacrificed his life for us.

Paul realized that such a great sacrifice requires a significant response from us. He understood how privileged he was to be chosen by God to be a missionary. He believed this was his mission as partial payment for the sacrifice Christ endured for him. He confesses that he was unfit to be chosen, let alone to be called an apostle, as his former life as a zealous persecutor of the "new way" was antithetical to the notion of Jesus and his message. Thus, he concludes, "But by the grace of God I am what I am" (v. 10). Paul's conversion and his commission came in response to God who first loved him. Realizing, as we have stated in earlier weeks, that responsibility and privilege go together in Christianity, Paul answered the challenge of Jesus by fulfilling his call as the first and greatest Christian missionary. Indeed, as he says, he worked harder than all others.

In the end, Paul attributes his ministry and his success to God, not to himself. All that Paul was given, especially his ability to respond to the Lord, has come from God. Clearly, Paul's message to the Corinthians is not only one of information, but equally, if not more importantly, one of challenge to respond to God who first loved us.

The scriptures consistently speak of our need, as Jesus' disciples, to sacrifice, to give our lives for others.

> *If any want to become my followers, let them deny themselves and take up their cross daily and follow me. For those who want to save their life will lose it, and those who lose their life for my sake will save it.*
> — Luke 9:23-24

Jesus is asking his followers to give their lives for the betterment of others. This is not a call to martyrdom, but rather a challenge to find ways we can use our lives, our talents, our opportunities, our time, and our resources to build the kingdom of God in our world.

The call to demonstrate sacrificial love is an everyday challenge to all, from youth in school, to men and women in the working world, and even those who are retired. Children have a special role to demonstrate love. Learning at an early age one's need to give up something desired so another good can be furthered is a fundamental lesson in life. Freely refusing to have some item, a new piece of clothing, the newest CD or DVD, some special food, and seeing in such action a solidarity with those who have little or none is certainly an act of sacrificial love. Children quite naturally form their own group of playmates, those with whom they desire "to hang," but sacrificial love means they need to be open to others. Many "outsiders" may wish to be part of the group, but because an invitation is never extended they can never break through and be recognized. Sacrificing for others means to reach out, as did Jesus, to those who are different, those we do not know, and those whom society has placed on the margins.

Working people and parents have different opportunities to demonstrate sacrificial love. While being a parent is certainly satisfying, this important task must be the most difficult work in the world, and one that becomes increasingly more complex as life becomes faster and more diverse, almost on a daily basis. Parents have been given children by God to raise in the faith and to educate in mind and heart. Such a responsibility requires sacrifice. Parents gladly give up their own agenda and often many of the things they would like so their children can have more. Seldom do you hear a parent not say that they want things better for the children than it was for them. Sacrificial love is more than giving up material things and time. It may actually cause us great pain, although we know it is necessary.

Tough love often needs to be applied when children or even spouses have gone astray. We do no one any favor by failing to address problems that arise. Surely it is much easier to ignore the problem, "sweep it under the rug" or do nothing. We might be able to keep peace by feeding one's addiction, but we are not demonstrating the power of sacrificial love that Jesus exemplified on the cross, the same love of which Paul writes in our lesson today.

Children and working adults are not the only ones who must demonstrate sacrificial love. It is a requirement of those who are retired as well. People who have spent the bulk of their life in education and work can now give back to society. Surely, the retired person has every right to rest and relaxation, but sacrificial love requires them to service of their brothers and sisters in public and private sectors. We can use the extra time we possess to help schools, both children in the classroom and other areas where our services can be utilized. We can assist in social service agencies for the poor and marginalized, such as a soup kitchen or a homeless shelter. We can assist our peers who might be less physically or psychologically capable and who reside in restrooms or frequent senior centers.

Sacrificial love, whether we are young, working adults, or retirees will require us to go out of ourselves. We will have to give up, as Jesus says, something we possess — valuable time, opportunity, or material possession — but the rewards will be great. Jesus says, "The measure you give will be the measure you get back" (Luke 6:38b). We recall Jesus' response to Peter when he asked what would be received for living a life of discipleship.

> *Truly I tell you, there is no one who has left house or brothers or sisters or mother or father or children or fields, for my sake and for the sake of the good news, who will not receive a hundredfold now in this age — houses, brothers and sisters, mothers and children, and fields with persecutions — and in the age to come eternal life.* — Mark 10:29-30

Albert Dürer did not know it at the time, but his agreement to go to the mines would not only produce a world-class artist, but at the same time ended any possibility he had to be an artist himself. His act of sacrificial love was an imitation of the heroic sacrifice of Jesus, which Paul describes in our lesson today. May we have the courage to do likewise as we continue to walk the journey of faith, one that leads to death, but eventually to resurrection and eternal life. Amen.

**Epiphany 6
Ordinary Time 6
1 Corinthians 15:12-20**

Raised To New Life Today

William Wilberforce was a privileged man. He was given a second chance; he was in many ways resurrected. Because of his efforts the world is a much more compassionate and just place. Wilberforce was born in 1759 in Hull, England, the son of a wealthy merchant. As a youth he led a rather dissolute life; his father's money allowed him access to people and things, yet he used his privilege to his advantage or abused it to the detriment of others. In 1780, he became a member of parliament representing Yorkshire. At this time he initiated what would become a lifelong friendship with William Pitt the Younger, who would later serve with distinction as Prime Minister. Still, he continued his self-indulgent ways; there seemed to be no stopping his actions that brought him further and further from God.

In 1784, however, Wilberforce received a great gift, although he may not have recognized it at the time. He met a group of evangelical Christians, a group called the Clapham Sect, who forced him to reevaluate his lifestyle. He was so transformed by his experience with this group that he completely changed his ways and became a leading proponent of social reform in Great Britain, especially the improvement of factory conditions.

Wilberforce's newfound Christian faith, his second chance on life, led him eventually to the door of Thomas Clarkson, a leading abolitionist in Britain. Clarkson and others were campaigning for an end to the horrific British slave trade that ferried Africans from their homeland to the New World. Through his position in parliament, Wilberforce had the power to do something about this intolerable institution. Despite strong opposition from many lobbies, he introduced legislation to abolish the slave trade and he reintroduced it for the next eighteen years in succession. Over time, more and more people began to join with the Clapham Sect and their allies, producing pamphlets and books and holding rallies and circulating petitions.

Finally, in 1807 the slave trade was abolished, but his work was not done. He became a leader in the Society for the Suppression of Vice, started in 1802. Wilberforce led campaigns for better education for children. He died in July 1833, literally a few days after slavery had been abolished in the British Empire. William Wilberforce was given a second chance; he was resurrected. Fortunately for the world he made the best of the opportunity God gave to him.

Wilberforce's ability to find a new direction, basically to rise to new life, stands as a good illustration of Saint Paul's message to the Corinthians in today's lesson. In chapter 15 Paul tells the Corinthians of the centrality of the tradition that he was given, namely the significance of the Paschal mystery, the passion, death, and resurrection of Christ. Now, he goes further, expanding on his earlier ideas of resurrection as a central focus of our Christian faith. This fundamental message of Christian faith is a source of consolation to us. Christ's resurrection will give us the second, the third, the hundredth chance. We need to respond to the opportunity of new life Christ has given to us.

Paul tells the Corinthians of his certainty that there is resurrection from the dead because Christ conquered death. This is the central article of faith for Christians. It is so central, in fact, that Paul tells his readers that if Christ has not been raised, his proclamation has been useless and so too the faith of those who believe. Moreover, he says that if Christ is not raised, then Paul is guilty of misrepresenting God, testifying to something that is not true.

The apostle also speaks of the essential need of Christ's resurrection for our future hope. Without Jesus' resurrection there is no reason to have hope in him for the resurrection was the event that secured our release from bondage. It was the action that released us from our sins. If Christ is not raised, one remains in sin; we have no hope to break the bond of sin that our first parents brought to the world through their disobedience of God. Christ's resurrection is our ticket to eternal life. Paul tells the Corinthians that if our hope in Christ is only for what the Lord can do today, if there is no possibility for future resurrection, then we are pitiable people. We have believed in a hoax. However, Paul reaffirms at the end of the passage that, in fact, Jesus was raised from the dead. He is the first fruit of those who have died. Jesus' action has brought release and new life to those who have died. The same can become reality in our lives today, as well.

Certainly there is no need to wait for life eternal to experience the possibility of new life today. As the life of William Wilberforce clearly shows, we can find and even should seek opportunities to be renewed, to be resurrected, and to find new life in our lives and that of the society and community in which we live. Yet, there is an important prerequisite; we must be open to transformation by God. Opportunities to find our proper road to God are given to us at certain special moments in life; they don't come every day! Thus, when the Lord provides the opportunity, we must be open and ready to respond. We must be attuned to the Lord's call since it is generally quite subtle. We must listen well. Remember the call of the great prophet Samuel. When he was just a boy, God called him twice, but he nor his mentor, Eli, recognized the Lord's call. Finally, when the Lord called a third time, Eli perceived it was God's call and told young Samuel, "Go, lie down; and if he calls you, you shall say, 'Speak, Lord, for your servant is listing' " (1 Samuel 3:9).

When God's call comes and we hear it, then we must be willing to respond. But this is often not an easy thing to do; it may require much of us. When the young man came to Jesus and asked what was necessary to find eternal life, in other words to be converted and resurrected, Jesus' answer was not received well. Much was required of the man who possessed many things. Mark reports, "He [the young man] was shocked and went away grieving, for he had many possessions" (Mark 10:22).

Yet, we have many positive examples of people, like William Wilberforce, who were given opportunities to change their lives and responded. The call of the apostles is certainly illustrative. When Jesus called, we are told they immediately left family, livelihood, home, and followed him (Matthew 4:18-22; 9:9; Mark 1:16-20; 2:13-14). Indeed, Peter was so taken with the miraculous catch of fish that he did not know how to respond. Thus, he told Jesus, "Go away from me, Lord, for I am a sinful man!" But Jesus told him that in the future he would be fishing for men (Luke 5:1-11). Saint Paul as well was given a second chance. Indeed, he claimed that he should never be called an apostle as he had been so fervent and zealous in his earlier persecution of Christians (1 Corinthians 15:9-10). Yet, God transformed him into the most famous evangelist and missionary of all time. Paul's efforts transformed Christianity from a sect of Judaism into the major world religion it is today. But this all happened because he was open to the call and accepted resurrection in his life.

Resurrection not only brings the possibility of a new direction in life, it also assists us to change our attitudes and perspectives. The general stance we take in life can be expressed by answering a basic question: Do we see life as a glass of water half empty or half full? The former attitude sees life in negative ways. We are never enough; we are always only half of what we need to be. The glass half full perspective, on the other hand, is very positive. This attitude places us on the proper road where we can make great progress. Rather than seeing things as lacking or inadequate, we can view life as fulfilling. True, we should never be totally content where we are and should push on to where we seek to be. But the glass half full tells us that resurrection to new life is possible for all.

Therefore, we need to approach life and the possibilities the Lord provides for us from a positive direction. Not only must we seek the positive perspective, we are challenged to help others to do likewise. Too often today people view the challenges and obstacles of life as a wall too high or difficult to negotiate. Thus, many choose not to engage the world. In these cases the individual has no opportunity to find God and thus the new life God brings. Surrender to the perceived inevitable problem will paralyze us; we will not be able to see our way out of the forest. Thus, we need to be persistent and engage the world. It will not be easy, but then the

Christian life well led should never be easy. We should recall how the famous British essayist, G. K. Chesterton, put it back in 1910: "Christianity has not been tried and found wanting; it is been found difficult and left untried."

The personal resurrection we seek gives promise to a collective resurrection for our world. If we start with ourselves we can initiate a tidal wave that can bring our world to new ways of acting and thinking. American society is dominated by the secular and a pervasive sense of apathy and indifferentism. Our nation trumpets its idea of the separation of church and state, but too often today this good idea, which was initiated to keep harm from occurring to either of these great institutions, now brings problems to both. The perception that the relationship between religion and politics is problematic has brought us to the re-exaltation of civil religion. Rather than honoring God, too often we honor the state, its precepts, and civic values.

The situation in our society, dark though it may be at times, can be transformed. William Wilberforce was only one man, but he led a campaign to transform the thinking of the most extensive and possibly most powerful empire in world history. But this only began when Wilberforce was resurrected to a new way of thinking. Similarly, we need to be open to God's message in our lives. The missive will be different for each person, but we all need to raise ourselves to a higher plane. Let us strive toward this lofty plateau. The goal that is our ultimate destination is worth every ounce of our effort. It is nothing less than life eternal with God. Amen.

Epiphany 7
Ordinary Time 7
1 Corinthians 15:35-38, 42-50

Formula For Eternal Life

George lives in Fort Portal, a town on the western front of Uganda, some fifty miles from the Congo. Like the Rwenzori Mountains (the Mountains of the Moon) that surround the town, George is a beautiful man in many ways. He works as a cook, among many other tasks, for a local school. There is actually little that George does not do. He is the one who washes, irons, and mends the students' clothes, cleans the dormitory, fixes what is broken, does the grocery shopping, and takes care of the outside yard. In short, George is a servant in the classic sense of that word. He serves the students and often the faculty and staff of that school from morning until after 8 p.m. each day.

He rides his bicycle to work over the dusty and narrow dirt road each day. He returns on the same road each evening after dark, a road with no lighting. One wonders how he can see in the pervasive darkness. But people in many similar regions of the world always say, "Oh people here know the area." One wonders how well he knows the ruts and chuck holes in the road that seek to swallow one who might walk the path, let alone dare to jog or ride a bike along the same road.

A visit to George's home would be a true experience for most Americans. In order to arrive one must first take that dirty and rut-filled road for more than one mile. Then you must veer off into a wooded and tropical land with no path at all. You simply have to know the way. When you arrive, you see an adobe shack of no more than 300 square feet. The walls on the inside are covered with newsprint; a cloth separates the two rooms of the home. The bathroom, if you could call it that, is outside, as is the kitchen, along with the chicken coop. There is no running water, no electricity, and no heat. However, George is lucky; his house has a tin roof.

In the main room there is a hanging string of Christmas lights. One might naturally ask how the lights are lit since there is no power. The answer is as simple as George's entire existence; he uses batteries. The home is filled with holy cards of saints and popes, rosaries, and other religious reminders. George lives in this house with his wife and five children, ages fourteen to one year. George has very little, or so it seems, but actually he considers himself rich. If you talk with George he will tell you how fortunate he feels to have a prayer life and family and friends with whom to share it. He is also grateful for the faith that was instilled in him by his parents. Believe it or not George is actually richer than most of us and he is grateful for it.

From a worldly perspective, especially here in the United States, George's résumé for life would not be considered very significant. In fact, most would rate his chances for advancement as rather poor. While I am sure that George would certainly appreciate having a few more things in this life, especially for his family, his concern is not on the here and the now, but rather the future eternal life which is God's promise to all who believe. Through faith George has the ability to look forward to his eternal life with God. In a similar way, Saint Paul writes to the Corinthians telling them that this life is transitory. Our lives truly are only a seed that will germinate and grow in the resurrection of the dead. He wishes to tell the Corinthians not to concentrate so much on our lives today, but rather to concentrate on a future eternal existence with God.

Paul starts his lesson by disavowing an idea the Corinthians apparently had concerning the resurrection. He tells them they should not be concerned with the kind of body they will have in the resurrection of the dead. Our earthly body must die in order to find eternal life with God. We do not sow our present body for the future; rather we sow a seed that matures later. God will give us a body as he chooses.

Then the apostle gives a series of contrasting ideas that show the difference between this life and the eternal life God has promised to those who believe and follow his pattern of life. First, he says what we have today is perishable, but in the next life all is imperishable. The finitude of this earthly life is transformed to the infinity of life eternal. All we know in this world is finite; all has beginnings and ends. But in the eternal life of God we will encounter only infinity. Similarly, Paul says in this life our body is sown in dishonor; we stand and make mistakes. In the life of resurrection, however, our body will live in glory. As finite human beings we are beset by weakness. Paul knew this very well. He wrote to the Corinthians: "I came to you in weakness and in fear and in much trembling" (1 Corinthians 2:3). Yet, in the resurrection of the just, we will gain great power.

In summary, Paul says we have a physical body now, but in the life to come we will have a spiritual body. We must experience the physical in order to find the spiritual. For Paul this transition is one of natural maturation. As neophytes of the "new way," the Corinthians are on the level of the physical. With time, knowledge, and the development of their faith they will find a spiritual sense of their existence. This will find its culmination in the eternal life of God. He illustrates his point by comparing the first man, Adam, who was physical and made from the dust of the earth, with Jesus, the man from heaven. As we start in a physical sense like Adam, we will one day come to a spiritual sense, as Jesus. He concludes by saying that flesh and all that is perishable is not found in the resurrection. Rather the imperishable, namely that of Christ, is found in the resurrection.

Our movement from the physical to the spiritual requires us to consider our preparation for this great event. Imagine picking up the Sunday paper, opening it and reading in giant, bold letters, **Jesus Christ Will Return In Two Weeks!** What would we do? How would we react to this astonishing information? I think there would be two basic reactions. Some of us, out of fear, would change our lives immediately. The Lord is coming and we are not ready. We might start going to church more often, probably every day. Prayer would become a much higher priority in life. We would pray not only in the morning and evening, but many times each day. We would seek reconciliation, with a member of our family, neighbor, coworker, and certainly with God.

Others might have a very different response. Some of us might do nothing differently. Some in a defeatist attitude might say, "There is nothing I can do at this late hour. God has already decided my fate. I might as well continue what I have been doing all along." There are still others who might not change a thing that they are doing, but not in a defeatist mode. Some could hopefully say, "Isn't this the event for which the world has been waiting? Isn't this the reason for which I came into the world?" Possession of such an attitude would allow us to continue doing what we have always been doing, confident that our preparations have been sound.

Most of us, I suspect, would be in the first category. As people of faith we have awaited the Lord's return, but we probably are not fully prepared. The revelation of the Lord's return would be greeted with much consternation as we would realize there is still much to do in our lives.

There is no doubt that we spend a lot of time preparing for the present life we live. This reality is part and parcel of our contemporary American world. We spend a lot of time in formal education, gaining knowledge in certain disciplines, and honing our skills in areas we have already developed. Generally the better our education, the more opportunities come our way. Professionally we attend seminars and various training sessions that will make us more confident and better able to do whatever our daily tasks ask of us. We spend a lot of time enhancing our physical appearance. Many people exercise regularly. This is obviously time well spent, and it helps us feel better and perform up to our capability. Others, however, simply spruce up our appearance so others will notice. We do this for gain today; we are generally not looking to our future life with God.

If we find ourselves in that category of people who are not ready for the coming of the Lord, then we need to start now to get our résumé in proper order, for as Jesus says very clearly in the gospel with respect to the day of the Lord's arrival, we know not the day or the hour (Matthew 24:36).

What needs our attention to prepare ourselves better? First, we need to review our relationship with ourselves. This might seem an odd way to begin, but if we do not have a good relationship with ourselves we can never progress in our relationships with God and our brothers and sisters. In this sense the parable of the prodigal son (Luke 15:11-32) is instructive. Before the young prodigal could begin his journey home he needed to realize his need for reconciliation. This process began with him. The résumé for eternal life requires us to love what God has created in us. Yes, the great commandment says we must love God and our neighbor, but we can only do this if we love ourselves first. Too often people show very little respect for themselves. This can be manifest in the way we treat our bodies through overindulgence of food, drink, or by driving ourselves so hard that we receive insufficient rest and relaxation. We need to take care of and respect our person.

Our résumé for eternal life must next address our relationship with others. As Paul says we are in the flesh, not in the spirit. This manifests itself in relationships that are fragile or broken. We find ourselves at odds with others and too often through pride we will not allow reconciliation to happen. Past hurts that we have inflicted or have been perpetrated against us weigh us down like a ball and chain. We are not able to move forward so as to further our relationships with others. The solution is simple, yet so very hard to affect: We must break the chain that holds us to the past. Jesus expressed this so powerfully when he raised his friend Lazarus from the dead: "Unbind him, and let him go" (John 11:44b). Once we are free from the past we can move forward and prepare our relationship with others and add to our résumé for eternal life.

The last and obviously most important element of our preparation of the résumé for eternal life is our relationship with God. We can build our relationship with the Lord in many ways. First, we must be in daily communication with God through prayer. The busy lives we lead can produce excuses for why we cannot find time to pray. But like the many things we "put off" in life, this is an excuse; priorities simply need to be set so that our daily conversation with God is never left out. Once we have established this ongoing conversation with God, when we speak with and listen to God, then we must have sufficient courage to act upon what God says. God generally does not hand us a blueprint for our life that precisely tells us what we must do. Rather, God speaks in subtle ways through the words and actions of others in the progress of our daily lives. But God does speak; he answers our prayers. We, therefore, must have the courage to respond so as to build our résumé for eternal life.

Our very comfortable first-world, twenty-first-century American existence presents a challenge to Christians. We live in the here and now; we seldom think about our future or eternal existence with God. Therefore, quite naturally we spend a lot of time, energy, and effort in building our résumé for life. Yet, when we observe the simplicity of one like George who lives not for today but for his future existence with God, we are reminded of what is truly important. Saint Paul in today's lesson forcefully contrasts our life today, one that is of the flesh, timely, and weak, with that of our ultimate life of God, which is spiritual, timeless, and powerful. We need to live in this world and do our best each and every day. God has given us talents and opportunities for this pursuit. Yet, we ultimately must find our life with God. Thus a résumé for eternal life is essential. Let us, therefore, consider our need to be more like George. Let us care less about today and build a résumé for tomorrow. The goal we seek, eternal life, is worth every ounce of our effort. Amen.

Epiphany 8
Ordinary Time 8
1 Corinthians 15:51-58

Christ: The Victor Over Death

In many ways, Nicholas Green was an ordinary seven-year-old boy, but he became a source of life for seven people and a beacon of inspiration for the world. Nicholas was born on New Year's Eve 1986, a new bundle of joy to greet the New Year. Along with his baby sister, Eleanor, and his parents, he enjoyed life and all the fun associated with being a child. With the help of his mother, Maggie, he read all seven books of C. S. Lewis' epic *The Chronicles of Narnia*. He loved to role play and considered himself a perfect Saint George, pointing out to his parents that he was half English. However, as his parents would often say, he fit the model of Saint George more because he always wanted to do what was right.

When Nicholas was seven years old his family took a vacation to Europe. Among many places they visited was the beautiful Swiss Alps where a family photograph captured Nicholas in front of the fabled Matterhorn. Four days later the family was in Italy sightseeing like so many other American tourists. The date was September 29, 1994. As Nicholas' father was driving a rental car, a band of robbers approached in a daring robbery attempt. In the process, Nicholas was shot in the head. He was rushed to the hospital and after a short amount of time the doctors told his parents that the boy could not survive. He remained in a coma for two days, but the doctors told his parents that Nicholas was brain-dead.

Although the shock and the trauma of the recent days' events could not be calculated, Nicholas' parents asked that their son's vital organs be transplanted into needy individuals. At the time, organ donation was a rare event in Italy. Thus, Nicholas' heart, liver, kidneys, pancreas, and corneas were used to bring new life to seven Italians, including several children who were near death. The resulting dramatic increase in organ donations in Italy has now been called "the Nicholas effect." In a very real way, Nicholas Green brought new life to several people, but the broader effect of his life and the decision of his parents to share that life with others might be incalculable.

The story of Nicholas and his ability to give new life in multiple ways to several people is truly inspiring. The selfless act of grieving parents who had lost their son was a true act of charity and love. More directly their decision to utilize Nicholas to assist others shows how new life can come in the midst of death and darkness. Thus, this heartwarming story serves as an excellent illustration of Saint Paul's message to the Corinthians in today's lesson — that Christ is the one who conquers death and brings new life. We can be confident that Jesus will bring new life to us. We, in turn, must do what we can, in our limited and finite ways, to bring new life to others.

In today's lesson, Paul continues his basic resurrection theme that he has expressed throughout the whole of 1 Corinthians, chapter 15. We first heard of the resurrection of Christ. We were taught that Jesus' death and resurrection was a supreme sacrifice of love for us. As Christ so sacrificed for us, so must we be willing to sacrifice ourselves, our material possessions, personal needs, and opportunities for the betterment of all. In this way we build the kingdom of God in our world. We were challenged to see the new life Jesus can give us and how we must adequately and properly prepare for this great event. The résumés for life today and for eternal life tomorrow are very difficult. We must spend as much time if not more on the latter if we are to find God at the end of our days. Today Paul concludes his message of new life by saying Jesus is the one who brings victory over death, transforming the perishable into the imperishable, mortal into immortal. As Paul says, God gives us victory through Jesus Christ.

Paul speaks of the new reality we will find at the resurrection of the dead. At the sound of God's command the dead will rise. As Nicholas gave new life to so many, so Christ will transform what is mortal and perishable about us into the immortality of God. Death will have no power; death will be vanquished. God's victory will prevail. The sting of death, namely sin, will be routed by God. Sin and death will no longer have power over us.

Paul concludes by saying that people must be steadfast in the Lord. If we remain faithful to God's command, our labor will not be in vain. Rather, to the contrary, we will move forward in our common efforts to build God's kingdom in our world.

Transforming hopeless situations into ones that find and generate life is not always easy, but there is ample evidence that such events have happened numerous times. Nicholas' story is rather dramatic in that through death he brought victory to so many. He made the impossible possible for others. History presents us with numerous examples of life and victory springing from the clutches of defeat and death. In the history of warfare this is certainly true. How was it in 480 BCE that a vastly inferior force of some 300 Spartans and about 1,000 other allies was able to hold off the entire Persian army at Thermopylae?

While the Persians eventually won the battle, the courage of the Greeks, the casualties they inflicted upon the Persians, and most importantly the time the battle consumed, afforded the Greeks time to consolidate their forces in order to win a decisive naval battle at Salamis. This brought Greece victory in the Greco-Persian War and halted the expansion of the Persian empire into Europe. How was it that the upstart American colonies with a ragtag group of soldiers and without sufficient supplies and divided loyalties among their people were able to defeat the finest military force in the world at the time? I'm sure that most common folks at the time felt the effort was futile. Yet, the colonists rallied behind their leaders and after eight long years of war managed to defeat the British.

There have been some famous political victories that also probably seemed impossible. In 1860, Abraham Lincoln was basically an unknown person on the national political scene. All of his rivals in the quest for the Republican presidential nomination were better known and generally speaking eminently more qualified than he: New York Senator William B. Seward, Ohio Governor Salmon P. Chase, and Edward Bates, a distinguished elder statesman from

Missouri. Yet through some excellent politicking and a sense of determination, not only did Lincoln win the nomination but the White House when the Democrats split their votes between two men (John C. Breckenridge and Stephen Douglas) and a third-party candidate, John Bell. In more recent memory the pollsters and the American populace in general gave Harry Truman no chance at all in 1948. Most were calling New York Governor Thomas Dewey the winner long before the voting even commenced. However, when people awoke to Truman's upset victory many thought the impossible had been made possible.

Sports also provides some important and improbable wins. In 1986, the New York Mets seemingly had no chance to win the World Series. Down three games to two and behind by five runs in the ninth inning, the end looked near. But an error by Boston Red Sox first baseman, Bill Buckner, gave New York new life. They won the game and the deciding seventh game; they snatched victory from the jaws of defeat. In a reverse role in 2004, the Red Sox were down three games to none to the New York Yankees in the American League championship series. Playing at home to close out the series, the Yankees looked like a shoe-in, but the Red Sox never gave up. Not only did they win four straight against the Yankees but continued their winning ways with a four-game sweep of the St. Louis Cardinals and their first World Series in 86 years. The infamous "Curse of the Bambino" had been broken.

We will face many difficult challenges in our lives, tasks that may seem to be impossible missions. In the journey of our working days we will face trying situations. We may face obstacles that will not allow us to work as we want. Coercion, threat, or the temptation of reward may "force" us to do things in a manner that we know might hurt or ill-effect another. We may be required to relocate in order to stay with the company or worse still our job might be lost. At such times we wonder what we will do and what the future will hold. Families experience many difficult challenges. Some people are asked to walk the road of ill-health with a spouse, child, sister, brother, or another relative. Tough love may be required in our relationship with one who suffers from addiction.

Many people must suffer the pain of observing a loved one reject God and the church and opt for the things of the world.

All of us will one day face the death of one close to us. The church will also bring us challenges. We pray fervently to God for our needs, yet our prayers are not answered in the way or time that we want; we might even feel God has abandoned us. Sometimes we lose sight of the road; we move off the track or even reverse course in our journey to God.

We will experience difficult times in our lives, with our jobs, our families, and the church, challenges that may seem to be impossible missions. But if we, like Abraham, Moses, the prophets, and Jesus, can persevere and continue on the road, then God will recognize and reward our efforts. The task will not be easy; the road to God has pitfalls and obstacles. Saint Paul advised his friend, Timothy, of this reality, "Do not be ashamed, then, of the testimony about our Lord or of me his prisoner, but join with me in suffering for the gospel" (2 Timothy 1:8). But he also assured him, "If we have died with him, we will also live with him; if we endure, we will also reign with him" (2 Timothy 2:11-12).

We must constantly reevaluate our lives and renew our determination to walk the journey of life, which one day will lead to union with God. It will not be an easy journey, if taken seriously, but it is the only path that will one day lead to eternal life. Let us, therefore, walk the road; let us take on what seems to be mission impossible. Certainly the parents of Nicholas Green had no desire to walk the road that came their way, but they realized their son could give new life to so many and thus, despite their grief, made a courageous decision. In a similar way, God will strengthen us, reward our efforts, and use us to complete his work on earth. Let us follow the lead of Jesus. If we can, our reward in heaven will be great. Amen.

Epiphany 9
Ordinary Time 9
Galatians 1:1-12

Don't Compromise Your Beliefs

William Jennings Bryan was truly a man who answered the call. Bryan, who was born in 1860 at the dawn of the Civil War, was an advocate for various causes throughout his life. As a young attorney he pleaded the cases of those who had little voice. Because he was so well appreciated, he was encouraged to run for Congress in the state of Nebraska and won a seat in House of Representatives in 1892. This was only the start of a long political career wherein he never compromised his beliefs.

The economic crisis of 1893, which generated the greatest depression to that date in the United States, created a backlash against government. Bryan was asked by his fellow Democrats to answer their call as a candidate in the 1896 presidential election. The Democratic platform advocated help for the common worker and the promotion of organized labor. Bryan lost that election to William McKinley, but he was not deterred, nor were his supporters. Bryan ran again in 1900, but again was unsuccessful. He was unwilling to change his message to suit others.

Despite his failure to win the presidency, the fame of William Jennings Bryan grew. His speeches and oratorical style became legendary. He traveled throughout the nation to promote the policies for which he stood. In 1904, Bryan established a newspaper that advocated many progressive causes in promotion of the social question, which was a front page issue at the time. Bryan edited the paper and again went on the road to promote its views.

Bryan continued to answer the call as the twentieth century began to unfold. In 1908, he again answered the summons of the

Democratic Party to run for president. Again he was defeated, this time by William Howard Taft. Later, in the administration of Woodrow Wilson, he served as Secretary of State. But when the United States entered World War I, Bryan, believing America's participation to be unjust, resigned his post rather than compromise his ideals. Bryan was the champion of many popular causes. He led the fight for the popular election of United States senators, where before it had been conducted by the various state legislatures, was at the forefront of the women's suffrage issue that culminated in the nineteenth amendment to the Constitution, and was active in the temperance movement and fought for prohibition.

The final episode of his life quite possibly will be the one most remembered. In the 1925 Scopes Monkey Trial in Dayton, Tennessee, Bryan was counsel for the prosecution, defending the fundamentalist Protestant cause against the teaching of evolution. Clarence Darrow, the famous lawyer, was John Scopes' defense counsel. The famous play and equally popular movie, *Inherit the Wind*, tells the story of this famous trial. Scopes was convicted; Bryan had won. It was his last opportunity to answer the call. He died from a heart attack one week after the trial ended.

William Jennings Bryan was a man who refused to compromise his beliefs; he was willing to pay the cost, no matter what it might be, to be a disciple of Jesus. This account of one of America's unsung political and religious heroes presents an excellent illustration of the message that Saint Paul delivers to the Galatians at the beginning of his letter. Paul wants the Christian community in that region to realize that there is one gospel and the people need to be committed to it. They are never to compromise what they believe; they must be willing, as was Jesus and Paul, to pay the full measure for their faith.

As with his entire corpus, Paul begins this letter with his usual salutation, but with an important addition. He states at the outset that his apostleship comes directly from Christ; he has received no human commission to preach the gospel message. This is vitally important, especially when we read today's passage where Paul's authority has been questioned by the Galatian community. It is important to Paul's argument that he possesses the true gospel message, which he proclaims comes directly from Christ. Since those who are proposing an alternative gospel message claim authority, Paul must stake his assertion to have the ultimate authority and, therefore, the true message.

Normally, following the salutation in Paul's corpus, the apostle gives thanks to the community to whom he writes. However, Paul is anything but pleased with the community at Galatia. Thus, instead of giving thanks, he immediately launches into a defense of his work and more importantly his message, namely to never compromise the faith in Christ that he instilled in the Galatians when he formed the community a few years earlier.

Paul chastises the Galatians for deserting the gospel he preached for one preached by false apostles. Paul presumably is speaking of the Judaizers, a sect of the "new way" that demanded full adherence to the Mosaic law. It seems the Judaizers had accused Paul of preaching a false message, one not from Christ, because he suggested circumcision was not essential. Paul's opponents believe he has "watered down" the message to make it more palatable to Gentile converts. But Paul defends his position, going so far as to call his enemies, those preaching another gospel, "accursed." He says he is not trying to please people; if he sought simply to make the message amenable to people, he would not be a servant of Christ. Thus, he reiterates his earlier claims that his message comes directly from Jesus. By implication he suggests it is the Judaizers who have misrepresented the message of Christ.

Paul's message to the Galatians, that there is only one gospel and the people must never compromise their faith, has inspired Christians for 2,000 years. William Jennings Bryan was a fervent Christian as well as a shrewd politician. While his fundamentalist belief may not be popular today, it was his total commitment to purpose and belief that was significant. He never compromised his person or his beliefs; lack of popularity, negative reactions, or political defeat were not important to him. He never counted the cost of his discipleship.

We live in a world today where Christians are constantly challenged by outside forces. These challenges come in two basic ways: apathy and indifference. How often have we heard a person say,

"It's not my responsibility, not my concern. I don't want to get involved; other people can worry about it"? The challenge that this comment, so often heard by us or even one we have used ourselves, can also be illustrated by a little story.

Fred Everybody, Thomas Somebody, Peter Anybody, and Joe Nobody were neighbors, but not the type that most would want to know. They were odd people and difficult to understand. The way they lived their lives was a shame. These men all went to the same church, but most people would not have wanted them as parishioners. Everybody went fishing on Sundays or stayed home and chatted with his friends. Anybody wanted to worship, but he was afraid that Somebody would speak with him. Thus, guess who went to church — that's right, Nobody. Actually, Nobody was the only decent one of the lot. Nobody did the parish census; Nobody joined the parish council. One day there was an announcement in the parish bulletin for a person to volunteer to teach in the Sunday school program. Everybody thought Anybody would volunteer; Anybody thought Somebody would take the job. So, guess who volunteered? You are right, Nobody! This is the apathetic attitude against which Christians must fight in our contemporary American society.

Apathy can be a significant concern for all of us. Many people feel they have no voice, no opportunity or position from which to present their views or ideas. If people have no voice, we might understand why their attitude would be rather apathetic or possibly indifferent. People often say, "You cannot fight city hall, so why try?" Oftentimes people surrender, not only because it is necessary in their minds, but also because they feel they have no option. These people are apathetic; they have given up.

We will encounter many people who for varied reasons have decided that they cannot use their gifts, talents, and time for a particular endeavor. Too often, however, we find apathetic people who, even with the necessary talent and time, choose not to get involved. Why? Because people believe, due to past personal experiences or by observations of others, that their efforts will make no difference in the outcome of events. We must guard against this apathetic attitude, because it is a trap into which one can easily fall. When society continually tells us not to get involved or that our efforts are of little value, we begin to believe that this is true. We become apathetic. However, we cannot allow society to drag us down to its lowest common denominator that refuses to get involved.

Christians today have an obligation to not allow apathy to reign. Some of us may be leaders in business, civic organizations, or even hold important positions within our church. Whatever path we choose, however, we cannot allow apathy to move us off the proper course of right action in seeking to continue Jesus' work of building the kingdom of God in our world. People look to us in varied ways; we cannot let others down. If we follow the road of apathy, it is almost guaranteed that those over whom we have influence will follow a similar path. We must always be conscious of our responsibility to others.

The struggle we have to remove apathy from our lives is also found in the contemporary tendency to be indifferent. How often have we heard people say, "If I live a good life, if I follow the teachings of Jesus, what does it matter what faith I practice; who cares if I go to church?" This tendency in today's society has been aptly described by the well-known sociologist of religion, Robert Wuthnow, at Princeton University. In his book, *After Heaven: Spirituality in America Since the 1950s*,[1] he describes the transition in spirituality as manifest in the United States, from the post World War II era to the present. He refers to this transition as a movement of spirituality from "indwelling" to "seeking."

He suggests that in the 1950s, American spirituality in general was centered in an institution, a physical place, such as a local parish. People found their spiritual sustenance by attendance at church. Not only did people frequent the church on Sunday morning, but it was the social center of their lives. Christians were physically present on the church grounds for numerous events each week. Wuthnow then contrasts this "indwelling" spiritual idea with the more common theme today of people seeking spirituality outside an institutional setting. People believe they can find God and their spiritual sustenance somewhere "out there"; there is no need to seek God in a physical place or within a particular faith community. Certainly the rejection of "traditional" religion is a complex question and there are many factors involved, but in general this new trend is an example of indifferentism.

If we can conquer the contemporary temptations toward apathy and indifference, we will be on the proper road to never compromise our faith. We will find ourselves in various challenging situations in the future, many of which may threaten our beliefs and faith. We may find ourselves, like the Galatians, under the influence of an individual or group who will seemingly "convince" us of the validity and merit of their ideology or ideas. Although we see the conflict with our faith, we can still be swayed. But we must remember Paul's message that there is no gospel other than that preached by Christ. Easy answers and solutions are often proffered for the challenges and problems of daily life, but the Christian life, while not always easy, has the answers we seek. G. K. Chesterton had it right in 1910 when he opined of society's "less than positive attitude": "The Christian faith has not been tried and found wanting; it has been found difficult and left untried."

Let us continue on the road we have chosen, the one that leads to Christ. May we never compromise who we are or what we believe. If we can stand strong, then when Christ calls us we will hear the words that, in the end, our whole lives have been lived to hear: "Come, you that are blessed by my Father, inherit the kingdom prepared for you from the foundation of the world" (Matthew 25:34b). Amen.

---

1. Robert Wuthnow, *After Heaven: Spirituality in America Since the 1950s* (Berkeley: University of California Press, 1998).

**The Transfiguration Of Our Lord
(Last Sunday After Epiphany)
2 Corinthians 3:12—4:2**

Transformed To Christ

One magnificent, moonlit night, a fisherman climbed the wall of a private estate to partake in the bounty of its fish-stocked pond. He moved with stealth and upon reaching the banks of the pond observed with keen awareness that there was no activity in the bungalow below. All the lights were out. With a sense of confidence, he envisioned his fishing needs taken care of for the full week. Thus, he cast his net into the pond making the light splash. The master of the house remarked to his wife from his deep stupor, "Did you hear a sound outside?"

His wife remarked, "My dear, it sounded like a net falling into the water."

In seconds, the owner sprang out of the stupor and visualizing his pond completely devoid of fish yelled, "Thief! Thief!" The servants of the house, hearing the master yell, scrambled outside toward the pond.

The fisherman gathered the net as swiftly as he tossed it and scrambled to find a safe hiding place. The workers' voices were near and the fisherman's desperation knew no bounds. His eyes caught a glimpse of a smoldering fire and he got an idea. He gathered some ash and rubbed it over his arms, body, and face. He quickly sat under the nearest tree in a posture of one in meditation. When the servants arrived at the scene and saw the man in meditation they asked for forgiveness and continued their search. Finally, they reported back to the owner telling him that there was only a *sanyasin*, a holy man, in the garden.

The owner's face lit up and asked to be taken to the site of the *sanyasin*. Upon seeing him, he was overjoyed and demanded that the holy man not be disturbed. The fisherman's fear turned to joy and then to pride thinking how smart he was to outwit the entire household. He sat under the tree until the shades of dawn began to sweep across the night sky. As he was preparing to leave he saw a small procession of people approaching; they had heard of the holy man. Now he could not leave under any circumstance. These people had come from a neighboring village and with total devotion had brought offerings of food, fruit, silver, and gold to invoke the blessings of the holy man!

At this very moment the fisherman realized that if by assuming the role of a holy man he had received so much respect and goodwill, how much more respect and goodwill would be received if he truly was a holy man. So the fisherman who was truly a thief turned in his net and became a true man of God.

It might have been quite by accident, but the fisherman experienced conversion in his life. He was transformed from a thief into a holy man through the action of others. The love, respect, and deference demonstrated toward him changed his heart. He realized he had been deluding himself to think others might respect him for his wealth, but he came to realize he could be held in high esteem by demonstrating kindness and those qualities that label people as "holy." In a similar way on this great feast of the Transfiguration, when we recall how Jesus was transformed in external appearance before Peter, James, and John, we must seek to be transformed ourselves. We must see our need to be converted into the person of Christ. We need to change our lives and conform them more to the one whom we follow and seek to serve by our service to one another.

Saint Paul continues his conversation with the Christian community at Corinth in today's lesson. Scripture scholars tell us that 2 Corinthians is actually a compilation of at least five and possibly six letters Paul wrote to that community. Over time, through the work of redactors, the partial fragments of these letters were put together in what we today call 2 Corinthians. Today's lesson comes from a letter where Paul seeks to defend himself against the theology of a band of "super apostles" who have infiltrated the

Corinthian Christian community preaching a theology different than that of Paul.

Paul tells the Corinthians that they should not become deluded with these false teachings but rather must stay on the true path. He uses the story of Moses in the desert and his conversations with God to illustrate his point. He says that Moses used a veil to cover himself after he spoke with God so the Israelites would not behold the radiance of God that was imprinted on his face. He suggests that the "super apostles" have veiled themselves like Moses. They do not see the truth; they hide behind a facade of their own ignorance and arrogance. Paul defends himself against such an attitude by saying if one truly turns to the Lord, the veil is removed.

Paul continues by saying that when the Corinthians see the Lord with unveiled faces, in other words, without the encumbrances of the "super apostles," they are being transformed into the same image one sees without the veil — the image of God. As he writes, "All of us ... are being transformed into the same image from one degree of glory to another; for this comes from the Lord, the Spirit" (v. 18).

Clearly Paul is telling this community of faith that they need to "see through" the false rhetoric of the "super apostles" who have placed a veil over their faces. They need to remove the veil and be transformed by the message of Christ. Paul says that his message is true; he is not to resort to cunning or false pretensions to communicate his message, but rather he produces the truth that he received from Jesus. His conscience is clear; he is to carry forth his mission to the Corinthians in a manner consistent with the commission Christ gave him, beginning from the day of his conversion on the road to Damascus.

The Transfiguration itself is a highly significant event in Jesus' life. All three synoptic writers, Matthew, Mark, and Luke, tell us the story. All three evangelists connect it in time to Peter's earlier profession of faith. When Jesus asked the apostles who he was, Peter responded, "You are the Messiah, the Son of the living God" (Matthew 16:16). Now six days later (Luke says eight days) Jesus is with the three special apostles on the mountain. Jesus wants to show that Peter's confession has merit. Some scholars suggest the

Transfiguration happened just as it is described. Others say the event was really a spiritual experience of the apostles. There are some, as well, who suggest that this is the narration of a post-resurrection appearance of Jesus that was intentionally inserted at this point in the gospel to make clear to the evangelists' readers the message that Jesus was Messiah and Lord. Jesus was physically transfigured for a brief amount of time. His clothes became dazzling white; his appearance was translucent. Moses and Elijah appeared in conversation with Jesus. Then God speaks from the heavens, "This is my Son, the Beloved; with him I am well pleased; listen to him!" (Matthew 17:5b).

Jesus' physical transformation was apparent, but it was momentary and not permanent. But what happened to Peter, James, and John? Most assuredly they were transformed. However, their conversion was not physical, but rather spiritual and permanent. From this time forth they could never look at Jesus and see only a man. Not only was their experience of Jesus and the two great Jewish figures of the past surreal, they heard a voice from heaven, God's voice, tell them who Jesus was and their need to listen to him. Peter, James, and John had the veil removed; they knew with total certainty who Jesus was and his mission and purpose in the world.

The transformation experienced by the fisherman thief, the same one described by Saint Paul and that experienced by Peter, James, and John, must be our goal as well. We might not want to admit it, but often we live our daily lives with a veil over our face that marks who we are and does not allow us to properly see the world around us. The fisherman thief thought crime would pay; it was his perceived ticket to greatness. But he learned through the goodness of others the fallacy of his idea. When he removed the veil he saw clearly the proper road to the goals he saw in life. Similarly, Paul tells the Corinthians to remove the veil the "super apostles" have placed over them. Then they will be able to "see" and hear the new message of Paul. Peter, James, and John were privileged to view the transfigured Christ. They were transformed in their understanding of Jesus.

What requires transformation in our lives? For some there is a need to transform attitudes — toward self and others. It is unfortunate but true that too many people have low self-esteem and do not respect nor love themselves sufficiently. These people need to be transformed to look into a mirror and believe fully that the person they see is a son or daughter of God. Some of us need transformation in our attitudes toward others. We think highly of ourselves; we place ourselves above others. Such an attitude needs to be transformed so that the attitude Jesus manifests and describes in the scriptures prevails. We need to be humble and sit at the low end of the table so, if we are fortunate, someone will call us up higher.

Many people need to be transformed in their habits. There are things we do that annoy others. There are habits we exhibit that are harmful to our health. We know what these problems are; now we need to have the courage to change.

All of us, to some extent, through prayer, need to be transformed in our relationship with God. Lent is the perfect time to root out sin and do our best to resist temptation — those near occasions of sin. We must do what needs to be done to improve our prayer life — our daily conversation with God — and stop making excuses for our failures.

All of us must seek transformation in our lives; we are also responsible to assist others in their transformation. The people who encountered the fisherman thief were instrumental in his transformation. Their respect, kindness, and goodness demonstrated to him that crime did not gain him the greatness he sought. The people removed the veil from his eyes; he was transformed in his vision. Our transformation can assist others to discover their own need to be transformed in Christ. May our words and actions be transformative for ourselves and others. May all that we do and say give greater glory and honor to God. Amen.

US/Canadian Lectionary Comparison

The following index shows the correlation between the Sundays and special days of the church year as they are titled or labeled in the Revised Common Lectionary published by the Consultation On Common Texts and used in the United States (the reference used for this book) and the Sundays and special days of the church year as they are titled or labeled in the Revised Common Lectionary used in Canada.

Revised Common Lectionary	Canadian Revised Common Lectionary
Advent 1	Advent 1
Advent 2	Advent 2
Advent 3	Advent 3
Advent 4	Advent 4
Christmas Eve	Christmas Eve
The Nativity Of Our Lord/ Christmas Day	The Nativity Of Our Lord
Christmas 1	Christmas 1
January 1/New Year's Day	January 1/The Name Of Jesus
Christmas 2	Christmas 2
The Epiphany Of Our Lord	The Epiphany Of Our Lord
The Baptism Of Our Lord/ Epiphany 1	The Baptism Of Our Lord/ Proper 1
Epiphany 2/Ordinary Time 2	Epiphany 2/Proper 2
Epiphany 3/Ordinary Time 3	Epiphany 3/Proper 3
Epiphany 4/Ordinary Time 4	Epiphany 4/Proper 4
Epiphany 5/Ordinary Time 5	Epiphany 5/Proper 5
Epiphany 6/Ordinary Time 6	Epiphany 6/Proper 6
Epiphany 7/Ordinary Time 7	Epiphany 7/Proper 7
Epiphany 8/Ordinary Time 8	Epiphany 8/Proper 8
The Transfiguration Of Our Lord/ Last Sunday After Epiphany	The Transfiguration Of Our Lord/ Last Sunday After Epiphany
Ash Wednesday	Ash Wednesday
Lent 1	Lent 1
Lent 2	Lent 2
Lent 3	Lent 3
Lent 4	Lent 4
Lent 5	Lent 5
Passion/Palm Sunday	Passion/Palm Sunday
Maundy Thursday	Holy/Maundy Thursday
Good Friday	Good Friday

Easter Day	The Resurrection Of Our Lord
Easter 2	Easter 2
Easter 3	Easter 3
Easter 4	Easter 4
Easter 5	Easter 5
Easter 6	Easter 6
The Ascension Of Our Lord	The Ascension Of Our Lord
Easter 7	Easter 7
The Day Of Pentecost	The Day Of Pentecost
The Holy Trinity	The Holy Trinity
Proper 4/Pentecost 2/O T 9*	Proper 9
Proper 5/Pent 3/O T 10	Proper 10
Proper 6/Pent 4/O T 11	Proper 11
Proper 7/Pent 5/O T 12	Proper 12
Proper 8/Pent 6/O T 13	Proper 13
Proper 9/Pent 7/O T 14	Proper 14
Proper 10/Pent 8/O T 15	Proper 15
Proper 11/Pent 9/O T 16	Proper 16
Proper 12/Pent 10/O T 17	Proper 17
Proper 13/Pent 11/O T 18	Proper 18
Proper 14/Pent 12/O T 19	Proper 19
Proper 15/Pent 13/O T 20	Proper 20
Proper 16/Pent 14/O T 21	Proper 21
Proper 17/Pent 15/O T 22	Proper 22
Proper 18/Pent 16/O T 23	Proper 23
Proper 19/Pent 17/O T 24	Proper 24
Proper 20/Pent 18/O T 25	Proper 25
Proper 21/Pent 19/O T 26	Proper 26
Proper 22/Pent 20/O T 27	Proper 27
Proper 23/Pent 21/O T 28	Proper 28
Proper 24/Pent 22/O T 29	Proper 29
Proper 25/Pent 23/O T 30	Proper 30
Proper 26/Pent 24/O T 31	Proper 31
Proper 27/Pent 25/O T 32	Proper 32
Proper 28/Pent 26/O T 33	Proper 33
Christ The King (Proper 29/O T 34)	Proper 34/Christ The King/ Reign Of Christ
Reformation Day (October 31)	Reformation Day (October 31)
All Saints (November 1 or 1st Sunday in November)	All Saints' Day (November 1)
Thanksgiving Day (4th Thursday of November)	Thanksgiving Day (2nd Monday of October)

*O T = Ordinary Time

www.ingramcontent.com/pod-product-compliance
Lightning Source LLC
Chambersburg PA
CBHW071712040426
42446CB00011B/2029